T4-ATW-810

COLLECTED LATER POEMS
OF JOEL OPPENHEIMER

COLLECTED LATER POEMS
OF JOEL OPPENHEIMER

with drawings by John Dobbs

Edited by Robert J. Bertholf

The Poetry / Rare Books Collection
University Libraries
SUNY at Buffalo
Buffalo, NY
1997

Published by The Poetry / Rare Books Collection
University at Buffalo
420 Capen Hall
Buffalo, NY 14216
(716) 645-2917
please write for a complete catalogue

Printed by Dual Printing, Buffalo, NY

©The Literary Estate of Joel Oppenheimer, 1997
©The University at Buffalo Foundation, 1997
© John Dobbs, 1997

ISBN 0-922668-15-9 (cloth)
0-922668-16-7 (paper)

ACKNOWLEDGEMENTS

I would like to thank Theresa Maier for her dedication to this project. Without her effort the book would not have found its way into print. Lyle Glazier's generous donation has partially supported the publication of this book, and we thank him. John Dobbs provided the illustrations. He also provided valuable information about the poems drawn from his long friendship with Joel Oppenheimer. David Landrey supported the work on this book at the most crucial points. His photograph of Joel appears on the dust jacket. I want to thank Susan Michel, Wendy Kramer and Kerry Maguire, and Pam Rehm for help in preparing the text. Alan Gilbert read through the whole volume and offered many perceptive comments. Kristin Prevallet designed the book, and saw it through the publication process. Her work is both diligent and gracious. The publication of this book was a project of the Staff of the The Poetry/Rare Books Collection. It comes as a small return for the years of kindness and attention that Joel gave to us all.

TABLE OF CONTENTS

INTRODUCTION

ROBERT J. BERTHOLF

Even now, walking the streets of the West Village, I sense the presence of Joel Oppenheimer. This was his place. It belongs to millions of people, of course, but he gave it special character by naming its features so carefully. The people here maintain families, the varieties of human love, a sense of community, the passions for baseball, and a fondness for the newest restaurant when all the forces of urbanization and the tensions of city life force people apart and fracture communities. He followed the turn of seasons—daffodils at the base of struggling trees, shifts of wind from fall to winter, kinds of produce in the shops—all that within an endless commentary about how to maintain the genuine in a daily enterprise. His talking defined the spaces as much as the poems and the articles in *The Village Voice*.

Oppenheimer nurtured the discursive voice in his poems toward a paced deliberation of how he saw people, issues, and actions. His poetry does not rush to action. It moves along slowly, sorting out ways of approaching the center of feelings. In *The Woman Poems*, the process gets broken up into separate poems, each approaching the Mother Goddess—the source of erotic love and poetry itself—with honesty and reverence. He celebrates the erotic as an element of experience that should be released from concealing taboos as much as he celebrates the ties to family members and friends. *The Ghost Lover* rambles, perhaps, through a series of settings, each one revealing his views of uncovering new passions of love for a woman. "Adornment of Body Poem" in *Del Quien Lo Tomó* rehearses a metaphorical search for love and poetry together. *At Fifty* is still another version of the poem unfolding in many parts, this time a meditation on the process of aging and the possibilities of living and knowing satisfaction in shared experience. Energy and verve appear in all the poems. There are defeats, to be sure, but the poems for the most part convey a vision in which hope for betterment in individual lives stands firmly against societal and governmental pressures.

When Olson praised the early poem "The Fourth Ark Royal," he provided the permission for Oppenheimer to write discursive narratives. Unlike his fellow Black Mountain Poets, Oppenheimer was not a scholarly man, or at least he did not import his learning into the poems. Only occasionally do references to military history and architecture come into the poems as a counter to the pervading perceptions of how to live one's life in an authentic way in the middle of the municipal complexities of New York City. He was informed, but the information at his command was like the information needed for a crossword puzzle in the *New York Times*, erudite perhaps, but immediate and useful. When he turns his attention to a new line and a different concentration on rhythmic form, the poems generate immediate complexity out of ordinary experiences. *New Spaces* contains the long poems "Acts," "Cacti," and "Houses." By accumulation of perception, Oppenheimer made up the streets and passages of urban space as accurately as he made up the rural forms of behavior in the poems written in New Hampshire late in his life. That was another new space with new traffic patterns of nature to inform his life.

This volume collects Joel Oppenheimer's poems from *The Woman Poems* (1975) to unpublished poems written shortly before his death in 1988. Those thirteen years were very productive and positive ones for him. *The Woman Poems, Names, Dates & Places, At Fifty* and *Why Not* are all serial poems. That is, each of the poems in the book is a complete poem, but each of the poems is part of the whole sequence. The series advances by increments, as the poems engage themselves by ringing together common themes and images. *New Spaces* is the largest of the individual collections; it combines two collections, "Drawing from Life" and "New Spaces." The others, *Del Quien Lo Tomó, The Ghost Lover, Notes Toward the Definition of David, The Uses of Adversity*, and *New Hampshire Journal*, combine the pattern of the serial poem with the playfulness, and deliberate uncovering of detailed observation about living in and where he was.

The Uses of Adversity—a poem published as a pamphlet, and then reprinted several times—is the poem Oppenheimer wrote about the chemotherapy intended to save his life from cancer. That poem found more readers than any of his poems; it transforms the desperate action of toxic chemicals used to save life into a mock battle, ironic, witty, and painfully self-aware at the same time. In *New*

Hampshire Journal, he records the shift from living in a city to living in a rural community. The seasonal changes become more pervasive, so the sounds of birds and animals replace the mechanical, urban noise, but even then the perceptive working out of a relationship with the place remains the human concern.

A large number of Oppenheimer's poems were not collected in volumes. Though he filed some of them in folders, indicating that they belonged together, he also placed copies of poems in several folders. He had not arrived at the final ordering. In these, Oppenheimer celebrates important events in the lives of his friends, enjoys the happenings in his family, maps out the world around him, and refines the rhythms of the discursive style to accommodate his new perceptions of a changing physical and mental place. He was "a maker," as Wallace Stevens said of a poet, who turned "a slight transcendence" of daily experience into the dimensions of a poetic place.

The Poetry/Rare Books Collection
September 1996

Note On the Text

The poems in this volume cover the writing and publishing life of Joel Oppenheimer from 1974 to 1995, from poems printed as a broadside at Kent State University to a selection of poems printed in the anthology entitled *Poets at Work*, published by Just Buffalo. The full contents of the volumes *The Women Poems* (1975), *Names, Dates & Places* (1978), *At Fifty* (1982), and *New Spaces: Poems 1975-1983* appear here along with *Why Not* (1985), *Del Quien lo Tomó :: A Suite* (1982) *The Ghost Lover* (1983), *Notes Toward the Definition of David* (1984), and *The Uses of Adversity* (1987). *Generations* appeared in 1983 as a private publication in an edition of five copies. *New Hampshire Journal* (1994) was published posthumously, but the contents of the volume were defined by the poet. The contents and order of the poems follow the contents and order of the first editions of the poems. When poems were published in magazines or anthologies and not collected in larger volumes, then these poems have been included in the section entitled "Additional Poems." "Additional Poems" also includes poems written but not published by the poet in the period represented by this volume.

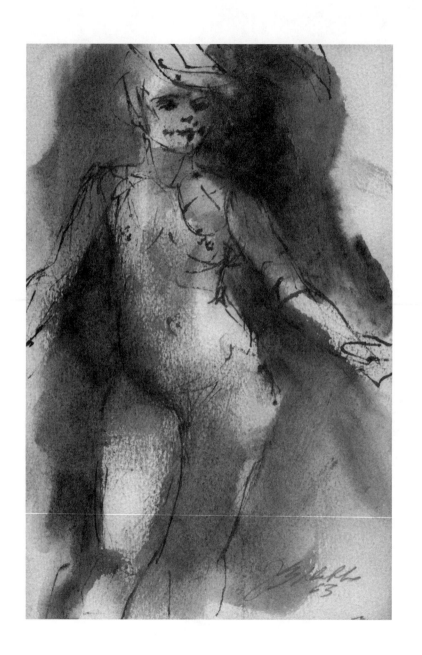

THE WOMAN POEMS

THE LOVER

            every time
            the same way
            wondering when
            this when that.
            if you were a
            plum tree. if you
            were a peach
            tree.

                        from *The Dutiful Son,* 1956
                        (written c. 1954)

EVERY TIME WONDERING

it is twenty years almost since
i wrote that poem, nothing
has changed, every time wondering.
i have changed, the cells in
my body twice over, almost
through a third, the object of
my devotion also changed, the
ways of love also, even those
sometimes subtler sometimes more
brutal having discovered both those
things in myself to a far greater
extent than you dreamed of. that
was mean who have dreamed more than me.
what i meant to say was i never
had a plan for that much as my
head demanded it and it is the only
unplanned venture of my life.
your cunt pants beneath me, above me,
next to me in bed or board, i do not
know what to do with it except approach.
i have no plan of action but myself.

if you were a plum tree. if you were
a peach tree. the line has changed,
even the images perhaps. perhaps now
i would ask for azaleas or exotic
tangerines. what has not changed is
the, or, the *not*, knowing where or
how in this matter painfully i move,
but move. if you were a tree which
had no plan but constantly to reach
the sun, constantly to hold off the
wind, constantly to flower and bear.
constantly to gnarl a little with
that constant fight, constantly
to show a sheen that shows you live.
this is the matter of it, what's
the matter. this is what we talk of.

GETTIN' THERE

twenty years ago i
knew about love. now
i am tired. i study
primary needs.
i wonder about cowboys
going to sleep on
stony ground, their
saddles their pillows,
the hard day behind them.

they twist and stretch
finding the curves they
will fit to, they fall
to sleep gently because
they are tired. the

way i am tired it is hard
to go to sleep, because
i have not been working,
i have been fighting.

gunfighters also go to
sleep hard, because they
are not cowboys. i was
referring to the working
stiff, the man earning
his bread. i was not
referring to the quick
dazzle of sunlight on
polished barrel, the
challenge, the long
drawn out stare, the
tension. goddamnit i
was not referring
to shots fired in
streets in front of
saloons, or tables
turned over.
                    like any
old gunfighter i
dream of the ranch,
working together,
going to sleep in
a bed as rocky as
the ground because that
is where we have learned
to sleep. but tired. i
dream of being tired
enough to sleep gently
and deep and not dream
hard enough to remember.

what terrible visions does
she have in her sleep,
my dale evans, who used

to work that bar in
dazzling sequins, and
also slept uneasily, and
is tired of it.

            we dream of
the sunset as the time to
lie down, we dream of banked
fires to be raked
in the morning not
night. we dream of
such hard labors without
tension that the
days of tension without
hard labors will
someday fade into the
sunset. then i
will know about love.

THE LADY OF MADNESS

i did not know what
madness truly was until
i heard the truth. she
spoke without lying calling
things by true names.
it was madness.
she said, you were the
ugliest thing i had
ever seen—i was
fascinated.

            i understood
that word as with a
snake. i had never
dreamed another would

say this. i thought it was
my thought, and
lovers, therapists had all
disabused me of my own
notion. i thought i
was beautiful.

                    she sat
in my living room and
with her crazy honesty
told me the truth. the
ugliest man she ever saw.
she was fascinated.
i listened fascinated
by her madness and
watched her body freeze
and thaw. she was mad.

MOVING OUT

because i was afraid
i hid from her. i turned
my face away so i
could not see her, i
covered my eyes.
i was more afraid
not looking than looking.
i turned to stone.
so i uncovered my eyes,
i turned not toward her
but not away, i saw her
always from the corners
of the eye, i did not
turn to stone, i moved
slowly, but i moved.
oh holy mothers save

me from your sister,
she sits always in the
corners of my eyes,
but i will not turn
away, i will not hide
my eyes. if she turns me
to stone i will stand
not moving, but i will not
turn myself to stone.
if she strips me bare i
will be naked, but i will·
survive. if she
strips the flesh from
my bones with her teeth
my bones will stand as
monument to her and to my
stand. if she bites me
in pieces, i will be in a heap
at her feet, at the center
of the cave. for i will
enter that cave if i
slip in my walking, but
i cannot stop walking,
i cannot stand at the
center. holy mother
of life, holy mother
of death, protect me,
i go to join the dancing
mother and i may slip
into the teeth in the
center of the cave.
this is the extent of
my understanding, stripped
bare, that i must keep
walking to find the
holy mother who sings
me songs, this is why
my lifeline continues,
why my fate line is

muddled, who shall
know which mother
protects me, which
guides my feet. i am
afraid of the mother
who bites, i move toward
the mother who dances,
or stand suspended
between them. this
is the hanged man
who was the fool, who
would be the magician.
over all great mother
sits while i whirl in
my head, it was pushing
that head that i almost
turned to stone, i
will not hide my eyes, without seeing
is more fear, without
seeing is no direction,
it is better to see the teeth
eating you, see the skin
disappear, see the
bones turn to stone,
than hiding your eyes
while it happens. it
will happen if it
will. holy mothers
protect me as i walk on.

NAKED POEM

you are so naked i
cannot touch you,
you scream if the
words are written
down. this is
the expected, how
will you accept your
secrets or share them?

i have come on
them in a hard
road and want to
talk about them, that
is a male deficiency,
what else can this
mind do with such
magics?

        thus they
will be my secrets
known only to the
world, while they
stay hidden between
us, as should be,
my muse, my turner-
to-stone, my beloved.

NAKED POEM II

women naked, men
clothed is an
old fantasy, we
dream it over
and over, bare
breasts frighten and
lure us, we remain
hidden, what will
you not do to us?

in such quiet ways
the world is
sustained, the
flowers come
every spring,
out of such lousy
weather, we are
out of the cave, we
are living in houses,
nothing ever changes.

SCREAMING POEM

the woman inside me
does not murmur she
screams. it has
been so ever since
i gave up breast for
bottle, the geometry
of shapes for the
algebra of numbers.
this woman claws at
my innards, sits
patiently waiting, beats

in my head, wakes up
when i sleep, occasionally
relents, opening herself
before me. i don't
know what to do when
that happens, draw back,
look for the solace of
straight lines, draw
plans all night on my
checkered graph paper,
plan out the rational life
of a man, and make no
room for magics. i am
torn by the ravening
screams echoing over
and over. love. love. love.

CHILD POEM

mother, heat of
early summer, smoke
in the air from the
fire outside, stretched
on my bed as a
rack at one a m,
she is half covered
by the sheet, her
left breast exposed, it
peeks at me, it
wants to wink, i
can do nothing,
i cannot wake her
for what would i do
then, there is no
way to touch, i
read my book.
he gives a piercing

scream, all fear, anger,
just once, but i
snap my light
off, hoping he will
not wake. mother,
i am talking to you:
was it you he
called, to fend off
danger, was it
you he screamed at,
frightened by your
look?

QUESTIONS FOR THE MOTHER

why did you make them that way?
why us?
what did you intend for us to do about it?
are you happy with the situation?
should we behave any differently in retrospect?
us toward them?
them toward us?
what is this thing called love?
do we need it?
what if we can't get it up even when we need it?
are there such things as aphrodisiacs?
are they addictive?
how long should it be?
can you tell by the size of their mouths?
or our noses?
or our feet?
what do you consider perverted?
should we feel guilty?
when?
do you love us?
how come you do us like you do?
is it all right if we just touch it?

DREAM POEM

girl of my
dreams i love
you.
          you keep
appearing in
the street, walking
by me, coming
up to me talking,
even sitting at
the other end of
the bar. in my
dreams you appear
naked or half
so, sometimes your
pubic hair is
wet, glistening, i
do not know what
with, you rub
against me, you
wear my wife's face and
body, you wear faces
and bodies i have
never seen, sometimes
i come in your mouth,
at your face, more often
i fuck you, sometimes
i am frozen, i cannot
approach you, i
am afraid. what
else is new?

MEAT POEM

we all know it, the
meat of the beloved
beside us in the
night, that is
how we feed, mother,
the feel of flesh
along the leg, the
belly, the arm
outflung to touch
the woman next to
us.
        we turn, we
move ourselves in
dreams, we hold
flesh to keep us
here. mother do
you not stand
at our side every
time we couple?
mother do you
not show your
face to me in
moments when
i least expect it?
mother do you not
frighten me
with your constant
presence? and your
demands? i hold
my wife's flesh, her
meat, i cry aloud,
mother do not forsake me.

QUESTION POEM

suppose holy mother questioning
you in my innocent
arrogance the sacred bull
is indeed the image? suppose
he does spend his
time in the high hills
foraging, growing strong,
coming down only to service
his hard-on? what then
holy mother if we find we
have perverted this
natural order? what if
the silence of cocks lies
around us because of it,
and because of it stone
mother is winning our
hearts and our minds?
what if we cannot
give milk no matter how
hard we are trying and
aren't supposed to? what
if we never mount again,
never paw the ground
lustfully, what if we become
all patience, all stolid,
existing only for beef?
will you be happy then?
will you be happy
holy mother or will you
wish again for the
bulls who came roaring
ejaculating over the
fields in their haste for
your cunt, afterwards lying
indolent in the fruitful
fields they have seeded
chewing their cuds? it

is in your power to
tell me. it is no
longer in my power to know.

BREAST POEM

holy mother now i
understand your nine
breasts, now i see
them over and over in
dreams, now i understand
the great sow, the nipples
erected feeding us all.
what i mean is they
move me, they draw
me—mother in this
season of the year your
daughters disturb me.

they run at me down bleecker
street, they walk slowly
across the campus, they
pass by windows where
i sit watching. their
breasts bobble and
bounce, i see them through
thin fabrics and thick,
i imagine them when i
cannot see them, i
dream of them at night.
sometimes they cover
themselves as they
near me, hiding their
breasts with their
arms and coats—whether
looking or not looking, seen
or unseen, either way

i am unhappy, either
way i am unsatisfied, the
breasts dance before me,
your daughters disturb me,
holy mother i am forty—
three years in this world,
what do you want of me, what
do you tell me?
        am i
hungry enough for your
taste, do i lust enough
for your body, will you
ever release me? will
your breasts ever dance
before me, will your
milk and your touch ever
fill me, will i
ever be able to dance
before them also?

MOTHER POEM

the first cries were
pain, the next anger,
the next, demands. ma
ma, each time different,
the succession of the
waking up. i went to
him to soothe him, to
put him back to sleep.
he was ready. he asked
ma ma quizzically, this
time for information.
falling asleep three
times he moaned ma ma.
this time it was loss,
this time it was

not consolable except
by sleep. holy mother
you know this having
heard it all your life.
do i fall asleep any
differently? does any
man? crying for you,
knowing we have not
touched you all day
long though our fingers
rake your breasts and
face, knowing we will
never touch you, missing
you, missing
what is within you,
in the slow creaking
rock of our cradles
or our heads. in our
dreams you dance before
us, in our lives we
turn away. holy
mother hold us
holy mother even if
we turn away, even if
we strike out at you,
hold us hold us hold us.
you will listen to our
cries every day and
night you live, and
we will continue
crying while we breathe.
a small child taught
me this, what has he
not taught you, what
have you not taught
him, what is it he
will forget when he
grows to my age, when
he becomes me, lashing

out at your dancing
figure, turning his
head, refusing the
only thing that will
comfort him at all.

MONOSYLLABLE POEM

holy mother she was
sitting on the couch
reading the paper.
a simple act. in
her short nightgown
her legs open at
the knees, feet
soled, so that i saw
her, the naked
underbelly. i am
speaking of the
fur, the whole sex
hidden. nathaniel
named it baby hole, i
the poet fall back
lamely on cunt and snatch,
pussy and twat. holy mother
in farmer and henley's
dictionary of slang and
its analogues there are
eight and one half pages of
small type to say what
i am trying to say and
that was victorian
england. under its heading
of monosyllable whitman
said bath of birth, donne
said best-worst part,
herrick the bower of

bliss, sterne the
covered way, rochester
the crown of sense but
also bull's-eye and
best in christendom,
chaucer the nether eye
or lips, burns the
regulator, jonson, socket,
and the americans, a
monkey. there are also
south pole and spit
fire, oyster, oven
orchard, county down,
cut-and-come-again,
niche-cock, receipt of
custom, privy paradise,
scuttle, seal and sear,
standing room for one,
sugar basin, thatched
house, upright wink . . .
holy mother we are so
afraid that there are no
words. she was sitting
legs open and i saw the
warm fur and wanted
into it holy mother—
as the spanish say
of it it is the
madre soledad, lonely
mother. i wanted into it.

DREAM MOTHER POEM

as i was sleeping
mother i saw your
four forms in her
body. i saw the
good mother her
mouth, the death
mother her asshole,
ecstasy in her
tits, and the
stone mother buried
deep in her cunt,
the teeth waiting.
this is not a good
dream mother.

TRAVELING POEM

you know that we
come to paths
we must take that
do not allow
for going back.
the crossroad
disappears once
we cross it.
in such ways we
approach nearer
or go further
away from you,
from ourselves.
the decision
must always be
made, there is
no standing still.
we crucify ourselves

on crossroads,
on your four forms.
we believe we
are going the
right way. we
do not know it
for certain. at
times we fall
into the teeth,
we turn to stone,
crumbled at your
feet. we move on.

MOTHER PRAYER
for nico dobbs

this child, this
child, this child, this
child. mother you
have love enough do
we. this child.
we do not hear him.
unplug our ears.
we do not see him.
open our eyes.
mother make the
touch come back to our
fingers that we may
feel him. mother
mother mother this
child is talking.
we do not listen.
mother you have
love enough do we.

MOTHER PRAYER
for rod rademacher

mother you take
the good and
gentle. you
do not need them,
we do. mother
calm this world and
our hearts, we
join you too soon.

LOST SON POEM

my son the terrors i did not
describe to you because i
did not think it necessary
have come to haunt us both.
they are not easily laughed
at or learned from but
what else shall we do?
does the moon fall off the
edge of the sky, does
the sun sink? all bears
are not pooh, either,
but it is hard to know
whether the real or the
dreamed are more fearsome.
if you live through reality
the chances are good you
will make it, while the
terrors fade. peace.

FATHER POEM

i have fathered
four sons, they surround
me in an age of
women, they will
have to fight like
hell to find the
action, i have laid
something very heavy
on their heads. the
youngest, perhaps,
will survive into
the new world.
                    myself,
like always and always,
i will be defeated, they
will carry me ball-less and
regal into the house of
the dead where i will
pay for this sin, having
fathered only sons,
having brought no young
women into this world.
but this is in me rock-
like, to do the wrong
thing, to pick the
wrong time. it is
obduracy, pride, a
need to go the wrong way.
yet they are strong.
it is the first time
i have seen them all
together.
                    i await
my golden throne,
defeated, regal, honored.
when i get there i
will have a drink and

let them do the fighting.
the fathers of daughters
cannot say this.

DISCOVERY POEM

lady, sister, lover, mother,
woman, i have called and
called my whole life for
your presence, asking only
that you visit. i have promised
faithfulness, i have written
as you tell me. they are only
words. when will you
live with me, be more or
less than inspiration? i
want to know those most
secret parts of you, and
let the poems go damn.
i want to fuck you as
li po tried and died.
i take my chances. would
you have it any other way?
you answer only prayers,
and this is proper. i
can give no more prayers,
and this is proper. i
want to fuck you, and
if poems still come
then that will be alright,
but that is secondary.
i have discovered what
is secondary, what is first.

WATER POEM

i water the flowers, lady,
i stand at the bar drinking
water, aquarius it seems
is a pisser. all things
grow under my ministering
save that which i want,
lady why do you do this
to me?
        when will my
own flower grow, pressed
between your dancing
gentle breasts?
             i
watch all things, all
things move before
me, only you hold
yourself aloof in these
dark days, only your
ass does not bust
its britches before
me, only you do not
allow the pouring on
of waters, only
you scorn my magic,
do not find my words
acceptable, do not
tinkle your laughter
like a fountain in
the hot summer.

FOUND SON POEM

if i am thunder
and i have married
all the wives, which
son of mine is this?
if water is good,
death is earth; if
the fire is
ecstasy, the air
is stone. where does
that leave this son?
how will i know him
when i see him? will
i ever recognize
him? will i know
anything about him?
will i stand straight,
my cock in my hand,
before him, just
as a father should?
will he know me?
will any of my
sons know me?
will the mothers
forgive me all these
sons? will the
sons forgive me all
these mothers?
i stand in a clearing
in dense woods and
am lost in the
elements. earth, air,
fire, water. they
dazzle me always,
and i am often
lost in them, mother.

LITTLE BOYS POEM

does the mother smile watching
her two little boys at
play? does the mother
frown, watching them
fight? does she see
them at all? she sees
them. she lets them
fight or play, ending
at logical conclusions
or ends. she does
not care what they do to
each other. she only cares
when they play with
her breasts, when they
stare in wonder and
awe at her nipples, when
they discover they
have nipples of their
own. she cares that
they know where they
came from, but that is
all she cares about.
she does not care what
they do to each other,
and this is the lesson of
international politics.

this is why the brothers
banded together. this
is why they elected the
father. he pretends to
care. perhaps he does,
at least enough to join
in the playing and
fighting. he likes to
win. the mother does
not understand this

concept. she is interested
in what goes in and comes
out, whether it is the
earth or herself. the
father and the sons do
not often even see the
earth. even oftener they
do not see the mother.
she always watches, but
she does not care. we
will have to write a whole
body of law to cover
this situation. in
the playing and fighting
man gets hurt, but in going
to the mother, he gets
laid. is this all she
cares about? one assumes
so, one hopes so. the
universe thus can move on.
the mother smiles only
when happy, frowns only
when in discontent. the
man has never learned this.

DEATH POEM

often men die in the
positions in which they
sleep. passing them on
streets, it gives you
pause. you walk on by
wondering if he's dead.
you go on about
your business. this
is the magic and the

protection we do not
have when agony is
involved, or passion,
or any kind of movement.
the body falling, the
quick drop, these
remain with you always.
but the sleeping
bodies lie, and we
walk on. is it
our mother's business?

DIRTY PICTURE POEM

when i asked you how
you could pose naked for
them and not for
me you said it
was art. when i
said i knew you
would say that you
said you were
swimming, only
your nipples
showed, floating on
top of the water.
this erotic image
destroyed me then though
you did not know it.
i lay on the bed talking
into the phone seeing
it over and over
as i have for this
whole day now. that
girl, also, for art
took cocks in her

mouth, this one in
her ass. another
swung on trapezes
jerking men off, art,
all for art, though
perhaps it is no longer
possible. you yourself
have liked your
head hanging off the
edge of the bed, you
said the blood rushing
down made it better.
you've asked for pain, for
tickles, for stuffing,
for pinches, for whacks
on the ass, for restraints
and freedom, blindfolds,
wired positions, and
multiple orgasms. now
i must wonder if i
will ever have it
again, and not only
because i can't
get it up. you say
you have changed,
and perhaps you have.
but if my hard-on comes
back? will it still
be only for art? i honestly
do not know and i
ask you. or perhaps
i want the sex without
fucking, for that too
would be just like me.
i think of your nipples
floating on the water
in the reservoir, i think
of the water lapping at

your cunt and asshole,
i wonder did your
nipples erect for cold
water as once for
me, or lie flaccid
like me. even dreaming
of such sights i cannot
raise a hard-on. what
shall we do, when
even the image fails to
excite, when all my
fucking is in my head,
instead of your body,
floating in the reservoir
in upstate new york,
breathing into the
telephone, instead
of my mouth.

BROTHER POEM

what do you know
of each other,
brothers? out of
the same hole, is
that it? fed at
the same tits, years
between, is that
it? do you speak
to each other? can
you touch each
other? and is the
fight against the
father, or for
the father, or
alongside the father,

all three straining
for the mother?
do you know your
brother better than
the wise son knowing
his father?

ceaselessly in this
universe is the mother

the great mother the
breasts and cunt of
she who bore you. you
will never rest easy in
or out of her, feeding or
lusting after food.

brothers you are better
finding your peers who
suffered the same loss
at the same time,
run with your own,
all of you seeking
the same thing in the
different mothers, only
the all of you have no
war with each other.

but you will
gladly kill brothers
and father and
sons even though it
gains you nothing,
even though you still toss
in your bed through
the night, turning and
seeking and reaching,
night and night

and night. in the
day you perform your
service, but not
for each other. who
can trust that much
and give to his
enemy? who can move
with his enemy
next to him, over
him, under him, who
can win the mother?

who will the mother
notice? to which one
will she grant her
company? her favors
being her own to
give she will not
bare her breasts unless
she wants to, even when
they swell with milk
or heave with desire.
to her the world is
populated with those
she tolerates and
those she does not.

remember this brothers
when you take your
first step in blood,
remember this brothers
as you lay dying,
remember this brothers
even as you plunge
your cock deep into
her, she takes whom
she will, she ignores
whom she wlll, she

has need for nothing
unless she wants it.

even the father fails.
even the father lies
dying. even the
father calls for
the mother. brothers
hear this: even the
father cannot win. even
the father will be
old and useless.

even the father will
have no magics left,
even the father's
voice will dry up and
the sons will shout at
each other—or
at their sons.

even the father dies
while the mother lives on.

she is old and the power
still lives in her.

brothers give up the
fight. she will have
none of you. she has
no need for us ever.

MUSE POEM

now she has shown
up at your house,
shares your bed, sits
on your shoulder late at
night. you write
poem after poem for her,
she is back. she wraps
her legs around you,
she holds you tight,
time and time again
you enter that soft
cunt. she will not
stay. at this very
moment, man, she is
here also, fucking me,
showing her tits in
the late summer morning
sun, visiting me in
my bed also. this
is how she is,
man, she shares herself
as she wants it, and
we snatch and
grab it while
she borrows love
and goes. all she
cares about is we
keep lusting, keep
writing the poems for
her. she does not
wonder about anything
except how hard it is
and how long it is
and how strong it is.
it is our cocks she
wants, the sustained

orgasm of our poems.
so long as we
understand this, we
can have her, and
she will visit my house,
your house, any house
there is that hard-on.
if that hard-on
is good, she returns.

we come down to
performance, despite all
we hope for. only now we
know what the stakes
are, we know exactly
what this mother asks for,
and if we do not
deliver, shame on us.
she will leave us.
that hurts, even
when you learn how
to handle it, even when
you tell yourself
you do not care. we
care, mother, we care.

which is why we ask
constantly for your body
not your mind. we
want to sink ourselves
in you as deeply as
the water, we want
you around us like
snow or the dirt of
the grave,
                we light
candles to you, mother,
we sing songs, we
even puff our chests

out, show our feathers.
finally we learn
to write songs
for ourselves.

which is when she returns.
and if we have learned
she hangs around some
more. she is a whore.
what else did you expect
from the holy mother
we sing to? what
else could she be and
be faithful to
herself? what else
could we love, and
be faithful to her?
what else could our
hearts break for?
why else would we sing?

CLOTHES POEM

lady why is it when
i sat down to write
i had to put on
my pants? tell me
if this was tact i
felt necessary, given
your touchiness
these days, or was
it protection, to
cover my balls
while the work
got done? is it
possible to do

this work clothed?
when will we face the
work naked again?

because this work
is such we must
set our own
rules, go by
sense of it, know
exactly when to
strip ourselves
bare, when to cover
ourselves totally
without ever planning
it or using it
consciously. after
all this time i
know indifference to
the body is
not feasible
for the poem
no matter how
cool we want to
be. it is impossible
to mistake the
swelling flesh of
belly, the swaying
breasts, the ass's
bend and curve, the
thatch of hair, for
anything beyond
what it is, just as
the dangle of the
cock can be, and is,
read as accurately
as any barometer,
telling the pressure
one way or the other.

i do not like having
to work with my pants
on—or off, for that
matter—choice, choice
is all i want and
ask for, and not to
worry whether my
cock offends you, the
possibility that
we came here to work.

TOUCH POEM

feeling you unable to touch me
i think of the times
that you did. feeling
you pull from my touch
i think of the times
that you didn't. i think
of the times i covered
you with both myself and
my come, and i think
now that you did not like
it, but i did not know
that then. i thought
it was a gift i was
giving you and it was
only your due, so now
there is no gift
you will accept. i feel
you pull from my
touch, when once you
pulled my touch
toward you. where is

the blame for these
changes, in me or
my love? when will those
touches meet again in
the dark night, in
the bed, in passing,
when will our eyes also
touch as hands,
when will i rub
my come on your tits,
tug at the hair of
your snatch, feel
your lips on my
body, my legs, and
my cock, feel my cock
push inside you, feel
you rise to that
touching, feel you make
me rise to your
touching, find ourselves
tying life and death and
ecstasy and fear into
one knot. when
will this house glow
with our lust, with
our fucking, our
touching, our love,
our loss, life, death,
truth, lies, come and
sweat soaking both
of us, head and
toe, with a touch.

TANGO POEM I

he keeps calling
the name of the
son when he is
coming in her ass
or her hands or her
cunt. what is he
saying? i have
called if at all
on the father.
even in orgasm we
will not let her
have dominion
or be satisfied.
what names does
she call? are we
to suppose she
also gets no
answer? neither the
father, the son, nor
the mother answer
when we call, peace
or not is only our
doing, we meet or
we don't, we
fall back relieved
or into the same
ritual we began
from, the only
sense if you call
for a logic being
to remain silent,
and breathing.

TANGO POEM II

or do the dance,
whatever its ritual.
it calls for no speech
when it is done for
itself. but the
problem for us to
whom it is not
natural is that it
so rarely is done
for itself, rather always
for us or me or you.
i spun arabesques
upon my heels the
first time i courted
you, and they were
fakes. they were done
to catch your eye and
make you pay
attention. when you
did, i stopped and
started whispering
sweet nothings
in your ear, and then
i tried to fuck you.
so that the dance became
the game we played, and
i never knew you
might believe it.
now i do. i can
do nothing about
it. i do not
dance for pleasure,
and have no way
to learn that now.
you will have to
take my mouth's words then
instead of dancing

feet if you want
what is of value.
the rest is forced.
but don't the words
anyhow mean anything
to you? don't they also
sway you so that you
can do the dance?
someone has to
make the words.
someone has to
say them. i
thought that i
would do. i
thought we could
come without moving.

MIRROR POEM

women i love and
watch these days walking
around mirrors bits of
glass in their sleeves,
their shoulders, set
glinting in light and
sunlight, in dark
corners of bars, medusa
i think of, the
stone mother only
approached through the
safety of mirrors to
look on her with
open eye straight you
turned to stone, stone
mother did this, stone
mother i know, why

are these women wearing
mirrors bits of
glass in their
sleeves set on their
handsome rounded
shoulders, to keep
my eye glancing
off? to distract
me? to lure me
on? that is
unlikely. they
are mirrors, mirrors
keep you from real
objects, objects are
real but not in
mirrors, your
hand slides over
the surface, quicksilver
was what they used
to make mirrors
from in alchemy.

as if in a stone
set polished in your
belly or your
touch i was to see
the world, when i
ought to be looking
direct. your belly
button straight into
where you live. no
stone. no mirror.

is this the totem
of their being?
mirrors? stones?
i tremble as i
walk, as i look in

dark corners of
the bar, light
corners of the house.

how came this
mother to my life?
how came medusa? i
tremble as i walk and
look. it was her
sister. it was
her sister. i wanted
her sister. i thought
her sister was here
beside me. i will
fall, turned to
stone, and cannot
move. the mirrors
are my signal who
she is, always. if
it was only my
wife alone i would
not worry, would
consider it fashion.

it is so many women
i look at these days,
mirrors flash and
blind me, stop
me cold as stone.

OLD MAN POEM

in the movie the
old man goes to
bed painfully, he
has trouble lifting
his legs. mine start
to ache. the hip
as i go up the stairs
is painful and i
favor it. my ears
are not so acute
anymore. squinting
i wonder why there
is never enough
light. and i keep
forgetting. old men
mumble their jaws.
my last teeth are
gone, the jaws
finally empty. you
roar and beg, roar
and beg, in the end
you are an old man.

stone mother takes
your body, your
muscles don't
work, your joints
lock, you freeze
solid in fact, like
she promised—all
for looking at that
cunt full of
teeth and the
hair made of snakes,
bosom of stone.
why did you want it?

why did you roar as
you chased it, why
did you beg?
                    and her
sister of ecstasy has
taken your ears so
what gain is that—
having heard the
song over and over
you now hear nothing.
the dance goes on,
but you can't hear
the heart pumping the
blood through her
veins or yours.

and looking on death
blinds you to the
world, she smiles,
knowing she does not
have long to wait before
you are young and
passionate again
at least for her.

and all good mother
has taken is your
mind, wrapped it in
fogs of thought out
of which you cannot
come. nothing exists
now except moments
from the past and
this present second.
which is not to say
i am dying, but
i do grow old, i
slow down, and my

cock hangs limp
between my thighs,
my head hangs limp
between my shoulders,
my heart hangs limp
in my breast. do
not pity the old men
but thank them.
soon they will ask for
forgiveness themselves.
soon they will die.
soon the sons will
grow old. only the
mothers will not
die or grow old.

i see the old men
sitting in parks
struggling to
bed struggling to
walk struggling
to talk. my heart
goes out to them
but they do not
need me. they need
the daughters of
the mothers is all
if there is that much
kindness.
                    hear me
you four mothers and
help them, and help
me when my time comes
also, as i have thought
to help you by
my service when young.
this is my asking.

NATURAL ORDER POEM

the spring king is
crazy and dying
long live good mother

the thunder god is
blind and dying
how shall he aim the bolts
long live death mother

the sea god is
stilled, not moving, dying
long live stone mother

the god of below the earth
is deaf he cannot hear the flowers growing
long live the mother of ecstasy

long live all the mothers, the four sisters, the daughters,
the wives, the lovers, the holders to bosoms, the thrusters away,
we who must die salute you

YOUR TITS POEM

blocking every time
i sit down to
write this poem. losing
sight of what is
otherwise always in
my sight, always.

the other morning
you said they are
big this morning.
they were. i was aware

of them for hours
as you moved through
this house, waking,
breakfast, the whole
morning.
                still i
could not write
the poem then either.

sometimes they are
defeated, they hang sad
and for that time
useless, they stay
bags of flesh built
to carry milk my old
art teacher used to say.
what did he know?
sometimes i can hardly
feel them pressed
between us, sometimes
conversely they are
pillows, we both ride
on them as we embrace
standing. lying down
they shift also, hang
to the sides or
perk out. they are the
most changeable part of
your changeable body. in
cold weather or with
excitement the
nipples erect. with
cold weather the
scrotum contracts. these
are simple enough facts.
we do not consider them.
your girl friend wore
bandaids to counteract

the air-conditioning's
chill in summer. we
laughed at that fact.
marilyn was very aware
of her breasts. i
should have shown her
her poem. i didn't.

your breasts loom in
my life whether or not
you like or can accept
that. i think of
their softness, and
their weight. i see
them in repose, anger,
dissolution, love.
there are very few
ways i do not like
them, so that now
it is harder and
harder to see small-
breasted women, now
there is no changing.
your tits have become
a barometer of our
life which i check
constantly for readings,
storm warnings, hints
of cooling rain or
the mistral rising in
the south. tornadoes
come and hurricanes
and calm fair days
and ice. they pillow
between us sometimes
when we embrace
standing or lying down.
they look smaller

in your clothes than
when nakedly exposed.
you bend to do
something and they
swing like dugs. that
also excites me. you
used to sit above me
and they brushed my
chest as they swung.
you used to take my hand
as it held your
nipple. you used
to take your nipple
yourself. you once
came to orgasm
with the rolling of
your nipple between my
thumb and forefinger,
steadily, slowly.

the goddess has
nine breasts. some
respond to the touch,
some do not. some
feed the hungry children.
some do not. some answer
only to changes in
the air around them.
i shall have to
chart which and
at what times.

SEASON POEM I

the season is changing.
every three months
it does so. three moons
with each mother is
the allotment. ecstasy
held us all summer, and
death comes now in the
autumn. next we will
hide from the tooth
mother her cold winds
swirling round her head
and no matter how we
hide she will find us.

spring mother, good mother
bring us the light.
ecstasy mother i
swear to you if
you take me and hold
me next summer, i will
make it worthwhile.

the song of the braggart
man, yet how else
holy mother to have me?

PARANOIA POEM

i am afraid of them
all mother because
i am afraid of you.
i am afraid of
men and women mother.
i believe they are

all fucking you or
helping you to get
fucked. i believe
you open to all of them.
in the late night, and
in the afternoon too
i see you spread
beneath them, mouthing
them, taking their cocks
in your hands. if
i satisfy you i believe
you want more, if i do
not i believe you go
looking. and of course
my brothers like myself
do not need to be
looked for, we are
always available.

they will lay hands
on you without the
asking, and quicker
when you want them.

as if it is loss
i am worrying about,
that someone else
should make you happy.
what i fear is the
extension of time until
you have no time for me.

when you go out
of this house i wonder
if you will come back.
is that why the catholics
light candles to you,
as a magic and a

signal? will they
lead you back? there
is no guarantee of your
coming and we all sit
sweating it out, afraid
we will be left alone
and hunting again.

that hunt is tiring, it
takes every bit of
strength we possess. it
grabs us night and
day, it gets into every
thought, until we are
left only our cocks
and our brains go limp.

they will all take
you from me, each has
something to offer i
do not, even your sisters.
their tongues peek out,
their bodies too, i see them.

don't lie to me holy
mother you would fuck
every one of us and
you even admit it.

this is why the fear
is real, you would
fuck every one of us.

you talk to a sister
and i tremble. you
disappear into another
room and i look where
the men have gone.
i don't even trust your

own self, which can
turn inward—eating
your own pussy, caressing
your own tits, bringing
you something i cannot,
the god fucking forever.

there was a time when
i believed it of me
and so you did also.
that time has passed,
and now that i think
nothing will satisfy
nothing does. so i
search your movements
and your speech wondering
who it is you lust for
now, who it is you
give yourself to. and
i wonder what i am
allowed to take
and find myself unable
to take anything.

holy mother what we
need is a pledge which
cannot be given, we want
your body forever.
we sit in our chairs
frozen without it.
at the beginning
we believe we have it.
then we begin to wonder.
we want you to swear
we have you forever.
this promise cannot
be made we know.
we begin to lose you

and our brothers begin
then to find you
who used to live locked
in ourselves.
                        when you
are gone like fools we
find the strength to
go hunting again and
we find you. we steal
you wherever we can
and we break someone
else's heart, as he
sits wondering who
you are fucking, where
you have gone tonight.

there is no equity
holy mother since
you are never
satisfied as you
sit locked in your
own self looking
for ways to be free.
i think you also
would like an eternal
perfection and even you
holy mother cannot
find it.

SEASON POEM II

summer turning to
autumn and we are
caught between as the
mothers pull at us.

all set to shiver at
night the mother
grabs us forcing
sweat and we sit
panting while the
heat sinks in.
soon we will freeze.
there is never a
middle ground not
in this life not
one thing but extreme
on extreme and we
fight to keep balance
between them.
                  ecstasy
mother you want me to
dance, death mother
you call me to sleep.
i cannot do both.

LIE POEM

there are poems i
will not show you.
there are thoughts
i cannot have.
i write them in
darkness, hide
them in light.
there are thoughts
i cannot have.

i am dishonest.
i will lie to your face.
i will tell truth
in the dark.

it is all a matter
of timing mother,
there are dances you
do not want to see now.
there are times you
want to see everything.
there are times you are
blind. so i lie to you
in light, i tell you
the truth in the dark.

at times you
see better then,
even all-seeing.

i do not want
to show you now.
you do not want
to see now.

i will wait for
the moon's turn

that allows you to
see truth as i have
found it in you.
the poems will stay
in darkness until
we are ready.
then i will show
them to you
in the light. truth.

WEAVING POEM

she sits at the loom
quietly. it is the
goddess's work. the
purest perhaps. it
requires the making,
the putting together,
and the finishing off.
the fates did it,
then the wives. it
requires no death to
begin, it differs
from the manly arts,
where somebody dies
as the ending.
it clothes us in
winter, it designs also
the veils that draw
us in. in the silence
of the loom the world
is built—the only
time she could not
face it was when the
child grew in her belly.

the goddess will not do
two things at once.
into the stuff of the
world she weaves the
stuff of our lives,
the pattern depending
on her head as much
as on her materials.

the cloth ends when
it must beyond her
control or our own,
and we must cut ourselves
to it. she weaves
silently in the rush
of building to her own
design. that building
is wearing, the designing
is not. but she drives
herself to see what the
end will be, though
that act she thinks is
destructive. she sketches
new plans as she works,
thinking of what will be
the next beginning.

nothing is ever perfect
enough, still she
goes on. it is the
work of the goddess,
who covers her as she
works, and, perhaps,
indeed, no harm comes to
her then. is this
what the need is?

the need is to finish
the piece, move on

to the next. the
end is the beginning
as in everything else.
all we can do is to
watch, grabbing our
moments within the
process, dealing with
it with the father's
answer: words. we write
words while she weaves
out our lives. we
look back, while she
strings out the future.

she knows the end when
it comes, we look
back on it. then we
say we have knowledge.

we don't know dick. we
know only the words, and
what it is we think
happened. we were no
part of the process.

this much turned out
mexican lace, while this
is a very fine burlap.

LESBIAN POEM

in the dream you
sat by her as i
wandered over. there
was no response. i
thought to ask you
who was minding
the baby. what?
you shouted. the
rage astounded me.
the two of you
kissed then, awkwardly.
your lips missed
slightly on the
first meeting then
came back and locked,
it was more than
a friendly kiss.
i sat frozen, unable
to react. i was
being cool. inside
i twisted, and it
was not a turn-on,
though i have dreamed
before of two women.
that was different
i said the difference
that then i was
being performed for,
i had my own options,
i might fuck you
in the ass or
you might blow me.
now i was not
present, your kiss
went on and on, and i
was not there for you.

this dream hurt me
so that it ruined that
sleep. i woke sick.
succubi come in the
night and dreams
and drain me because
there is no other
way. i twist and
turn under their assault
and do not know which
is you, which the
mother, which the
woman part of myself.

i am scared, i look
for help. the two
of you were kissing
as i sat there beside
you. i meant honestly
to ask about the
child, but you
would not hear of
it, and went to
kissing her. i do
not like such dreams,
though we used to
joke about them.
two on one is fine
you'd say if there be
two men, you'd
not enough of lesbian
in you. this mother
is in my dreams
now, coming between
us. how will i
regain my place,
how will i replace

the mother in this
dream, how will i
kiss you again, on
the lips, our lips
sliding to meet and
hold. mother come to
me in dreams and
tell me how, mother
make your sister
disappear, give
me back my wife.

SUNDAY POEM

i forget what you
feel like. i
forget your taste
and smell, i forget
the color of your
hair. this has
always been my
failing, mother,
i cannot carry you
with me. each
time is a new
time. bending to
your cunt it tastes
as i cannot remember.
memory does not
ride with me.
there is no way
i can reconstruct
you when you go.
i cannot always
touch you, so
you are gone.

i cannot always
fuck you, so
you are gone.

cannot cannot cannot.
can. will. this
is not where it
is, this is not
where it should be.

we go day by day.
sunday mornings mother
i pray to you,
i reach for you
early in bed, i
think of you this
whole day long.
was my father
any different? was
my mother any
less satisfied?
why should anyone
else concern us?
i reach for you
tentatively, as if
you might be gone.
you might be. going
is not coming the
sage said.
        sunday your
body moves next to
me, we have nothing
to do but fuck.

we used to use the
afternoons also
and the nights
and every hour. i
cannot touch you

always, or even
reach you. there is
a void we cannot
cross. we block
ourselves and
pull away. the edge
is clear and sharp,
distinctly, knowing
what we're doing, we
avoid it. we will
not take the plunge.

on monday the alarm
rings loud and clear
chasing you from my
dreams. how did we
get to this abyss?
how do we get away
from it? still i
will reach. i will
not give it up.
how will i hold
you with me? how
will i break
this circle we spin
in? to find the
afternoons and nights,
the other mornings?
the dance will
begin again, we
will swing past
the gaps, we
will come through.
holy mother i
swear it to you.
i will keep on
singing, you
will still dance.

DEFINITION POEM

the goddess is
mother daughter
sister wife with
or without
man. each act
is separate and
contained. the
man does not know
any of them. he
clutches each
portion as his
own. what
does she care?
it is as if each
act performs itself.
she does not care.
he will suck her
tit for milk, he
will caress her
breast for love,
he will tweak her
nipple for sex,
he will draw away
in fear from
touching of her
magic. when she
is young and growing
she says where
do i put these?

PRAYER POEM

holy mother of the
perfect tits. holy
mother of the not
perfect tits. holy
mother of the body
which asks. holy
mother of the body
which denies. holy
mother whose arms
reach out to take
me, whose arms lash
out and deny me, whose
cunt opens, warm and
wet, whose cunt lies
folded tight in its
hair and its lips,
holy mother of all
the mysteries hear
this, stay with me.

in the end and in
the beginning stay
with me. there is no
end holy mother that
is not beginning.

stay with me.
holy mother though you
leave you are here.
holy mother when you
are here i am
alone. holy mother
you have nothing
to do with this.
holy mother i build
you out of my
own head and this
is my disservice.

holy mother i
have not trained
myself other, except
in secret moments
when i discover
the perfections and
imperfections of your
breasts, cunt, ass,
arms, et cetera.
in such holy moments
i have found you
again and again.
in the end
is the beginning.
do not leave me.

do not let me fail
in believing. holy
mother come to
me or wait as
you are i will
move. i will touch
you and hold you.
i will see you
at last. do
not leave me at
this moment as
you have left me
at others. do not
let me leave you
now as i have left
you before. let
me look at you
and touch you.
holy mother i
beseech you. holy
mother i pray.

holy mother of
the perfections and
imperfections let
me open your cunt
or give me whatever
strength i need
that i may leave.

in such leaving to
find you or make
you find me, holy
mother, because i
am hung at the middle
of the square and
the circle, i go
neither right nor
left, up nor down.
this is the service
of no one, this
will destroy us all.
give me the strength to
stay or to leave
holy mother,
give me the strength.

you sit silent
so that i have
only my own voice.
this is the answer
to prayers, the
end is the beginning,
the leaving the coming,
the perfection the
not perfect in all things.
mother gives and
mother takes away.

PRAYER POEM II

mother gives and
mother takes away.
mother comes close
mother goes far.
mother suckles and
weans mother
does all things
each in its time.

give me strength.

mother give me
strength or take it.
i do what i can
in your service.
is it fair to mark
me for this? there
is no fairness she
says only life. so
the service is
ended. to begin.
again. again. again.
the service begins
again. give me strength.

FANTASY POEM

thinking of all the
instruments that have
entered all of you
there including
this cock for your
or my delight.
                    the
clothes you have put
on both under and
over, the positions
you have taken, reached,
or been put in, even
the beatings suffered
or given.
                    which is
flesh or fantasy and
what is allowable.

baring your ass rosy
for the spanking,
parading in heels,
dreaming yes of
ropes, wanting the
feel of textures rough
and smooth against
you, how shall we
ever meet?

                    in the
mouth, in the ass,
some of you have
sucked my finger wet
from your cunt and
some of you have felt
the prickling of your
skin from feathers on

the nipple. one of
you molded butter in
your pussy to find
out its shape.

              or
were you just fucking
around? you have
turned me on with
clothes cut for
swelling bellies and
with leather skirts that
lifted off your naked
ass when you bent
down.
        why didn't i
let you blow me in
the bar one time?
why couldn't i
fuck you in the field
that warm spring day?
what clothes will
you wear in heaven when
i meet you with an
eternal hard-on? what
positions then, what
odors will we smell,
what forms our orgasms
take, what sounds we
make?
        twenty years ago or
more i pulled your
blouse down from your
shoulders and i still
remember that, a peasant
blouse, i see it, feel
the texture, see your
nipple as it came

in view. i see your
thighs heavy up under
you one afternoon, i
see the particular
dusty rose brassiere
you wore another night.

i lift satin or velvet
or denim under it is
always your pubic
thatch of hair and
the lips are wet.
you suck my cock,
your ass and cunt are
stuffed with vibrators,
your hands and feet
outstretched, your
eyes are closed, your
breasts have ropes
across them. you shudder
as you come. i do
not know which is
flesh which is fantasy
which was for the other
which was for the self.
i do not know why
shudders are both
good and bad for us.
do you suppose we
will know in heaven?

NAMES, DATES & PLACES

FIRST POEM FOR MY LAST SON

for six months
he babbled in tongues
now he speaks american

which is what you do
you filter out all
the sounds you don't use

meanwhile i take lessons
with the master and he instructs me
to walk like a baby when he learns
the groin relaxed and the weight
carried below the navel

how much will i have to learn
from you oh my best beloved
while my culture falls on your head
and exactly who will win as
i go down and you come struggling up

the race is of course to the swiftest
yet gravity is on my side at last
and you have only strength
and your babble is too light-hearted
to last
         you will engrave your
head and body with loads too big
and your weight also will move upward
into your chest and your air will turn bad
there is nothing else i can tell you

but even when you were
speaking in tongues i didn't listen
and i never know even now
when you are telling me something

and this time for me
there will be no next time
no new sons to not hear

i have lost it again
as with all my sons

but i will try to learn to walk
at least while you can teach me
but you must bear with me
since it is hard even though
i try my damnedest
                          while your feet
find their own ways to friend
to mother brother father
going to the wall for support
relaxing the groin and carrying
the weight below your navel
while keeping your legs fluid
and the air in you around you good

FIRST SONG AT SAINT ANDREWS

redbud tree
magenta
hard-edged
in the sun

pure magenta
startles

in the next day's
grayness
softer-edged
more a smudge
also startling

the center
carrying the force

redbud tree
from any distance
it is the leaves
one thinks
making the blur
of rich magenta
against the sky
against the lake

it cannot be ignored

actually small florets
ride each branch
profusely and
not the leaves
it is actually
flowers blooming
in the march air

one wants
a palette loaded
with magenta

the only time
in nature
it is allowed

not to mention real

one wants to sit
on the stone bench
squinting
                holding
one's brush
up and out

just like
a real artist

one wants
to use up
a year's allotment
of magenta

SECOND SONG AT SAINT ANDREWS

the flowers are
tiny and true purple
in the grass itself

mingling with them
even smaller
light blue-purples
spread among them
jump the path
and take the other side

what a curious combination
for this season

but just last friday
in that colder
northern city
saw first crocus spring
all purple too
in a single square
of dirt from which
ailanthus grew
that hopeless city tree
which never knows
any other color
than sallow green

or dirty yellow
under city sky

so, everywhere
purple, purple-blue
and such
for spring

E. P. 1885-1972

for a long while you
were owned by everyone,
an object, an
enemy, someone to
defend or excoriate;
owned but not sold
you said come my
songs we will sing
of perfections we
will get ourselves
hated; you said every
day as the sun rises
make it new; you even
said a long time ago
we elect either knaves
or eunuchs to lead us;
you were talking of
america; you were
not a nice man; you
taught us all the
language and you
reinvented the forms;
you lived these last
years in silence, telling
us something more; you
walked naked all your

life putting your
life on the line for
the taking, you were
bought, owned, now
you are dead and in
the perfect way of
this world, now
only the poets can
own you, barter
your brilliance in
their lonely rooms,
parlay your winnings,
fight over your
coat you never once
turned, now the
world is done with
you and only
the poets own you.

FOR CHARLES REZNIKOFF
1894-1976

outside the spring is here
for once calendar and air the same

streets full of people
coats open or off, unhatted
a field of flowers opening to the sun
spring! spring is here!

but he died not seeing this this year
he died in winter after many springs
but every spring he saw we see still
every spring he saw we see still

A LETTER TO PHILIP

can i any longer address you dear phil
when i have spent the morning
ordering my life in unrealities

the rent the food the clothing
the ten percent allowed for luxuries
the baseball register and the sporting news

which things are necessary in my world i say

i have written my oldest son
and sent a check to celebrate his nineteenth year
and i have yelled at my youngest son
to celebrate his curiosity which stalled my writing checks

my head is awhirl with money and games and family
and you are in the real world finally

now you are not only my brother
but the world's brother and the ant's brother
god's brother and even the foolish writer's brother

which is why i wonder how i dare start a letter dear phil
wanting to know the honorific when you must recognize none such
but there is a need to honor you somehow
as you honor me by every step you take

i think of you sitting silent sitting speaking walking
and i am honored
                    i have been given this grace to know a decent man
who does right things while i whirl in unrealities
writing checks and poems

COMMENTARY

> "Sun penetrating young woman's blouse, outlining breast
> reminds me of Zeus in love with mortal woman."

reminds me of me in love with mortal woman
and of better angles, and even, zeus forbid,
of the act of penetrating them

> "I find farting as a pastime just as rewarding as
> cigarette smoking. Besides, it relieves the tension
> closer to the center of feeling in the stomach."

i find jerking off even closer to
that center, and far more tension-relieving.
i find cigar smoking a pastime.
i fart only when i eat vegetables, or too much,
or when i want to make a statement.

> "Man or woman leaves bus seat beside me and i feel with
> my hands for the warmth there left behind."

man or woman leaves bus seat beside me,
i feel for the ass that has sat there.

> "I mistook a running motor this morning for a chirping bird."

i mistook a bird chirping this morning for
a running motor. I have been away too long.
i mistook a bee for an instrument of death.
i have been away too far. i do not confuse myself
by my own mistakes. i know when i am crazy, and
then take appropriate action. i move.

i will never have international acclaim in this fashion,
nor journals publish for everyone's enlightenment.

THE YELLOW CRANE
from ts'ui hao

yellow crane gone with old man,
this house was built in their name.
the crane gone never returns,
every thousand years the same.

by day: clear sky, stream, bright leaves,
sweet grass, lush island, glad song.
then the night: which way is home?
river mists, sadness comes strong.

VOWELS
after rimbaud

a black, e white, i red, u green, o blue : vowels,
someday i'm going to tell your inner secrets :
a, a corset of hairy shining flies, sequins
covering the stink of every body's bowels

and its dark gulfs; e, honesty of steam or tents,
proud points of ice floes, ermined kings, shivered star tips
i, purplings, hawked blood, the smile of beautiful lips
as in anger or the raptures of penitence;

u, cycles, holy rolling swells of greeny seas,
peace of full pastures, peace of deep imprinted frieze
on wise men's brows, put there by alchemy and scored;

o, final trumpeter, full of coarse stridences,
worlds and angels travel through your round silences,
o, omega.
                your eyes, pure violet outpoured.

HUNTER
for hp

in the sky, and
dog too
        hound
the other stars

sword lifted spinning
my sky
        slice the
moon in crescent
slivers
        you are
so bright we
see you circle
every night
                spring
comes
        the great
bear awakens
                hunter
be ready, dog
strain at heel

spring comes soon

SIOUX SONG
for vdl

it is raining
it is raining
we sit together
we sit together
the weather is inside us
the weather is inside us

POEM FOR THE NEW YEAR
31 december 1973

i shower carefully, scrubbing
my body, preparing myself
for new year. having been
a dirty young man shall
i now start being clean?
i watched your body while
you dressed. 'desire springs
in me yet, i ought to be
satisfied' is a line i wrote
fifteen years ago. now we
have grown older in our ways
and in our heads also. now
i dream of medusa, where it
was always her sister who
presented herself. now medusa
strangles me, and i am saved
by the old poet, he helps me
break loose. he tells me
he's never yet seen one would
hold on if you fought long enough.
i hope he's right. i woke from

that dream stiff-necked and
sore from the struggle, but
i had lasted another year
from the freezing of my breath.
today i saw a basilisk in my
dream who also tried to freeze me.
i woke abruptly, thrashing, safe
again, as he scuttled across the floor.
the basilisk does not grow
older, does not ever change.

we walk on, and sleep each night.
he said: hold on, hold on,
until the new vision comes.
it comes, it opens up,
it always comes. but some years
are long waits in which we
sleep and dream of basilisks
and mother medusa waiting
waiting to stop us. we cannot
stop. we cannot stop her.
someday we will welcome her.
medusa stay way from my door.
let me look once again at
a woman's body without the
mothers intervening, getting
in the way. let desire rise
in me still. i will be satisfied.

mothers: under the running water,
in this dirt of my life,
in the cold air of new year,
in the fire which sustains
and consumes us, bring me
to the next new year,
to the next growing old,
to the next growing up,
to the next growing out.

2/2/76

this day wet storm
moving fast from the south

very cold arctic winds
from north and west

no turning of ocean
no milding

temperature dropping
zero or below

wind howled all night long

could not sleep

poked my nose out
on errands early
no sun no shadow

later sun broke through
wind still strong
icy underfoot

in pennsylvania
he saw his shadow

six weeks or no

it is enough
as always

VALENTINE'S DAY 1974

listening to the stories
romance through the ages.
tonight i hear it again and
although we grow older we
are still moiled in it. is he
filled with so much passion
still, still unresolved, still
waiting like a lover for his
love made real? even doddering
will he beg her flesh to
take form before him, even
trembling with age will he
adore and lose:
                        laughing
and crying i listen. a
poet has only his ears.
i am glad he is still
passionate. i cry out my
own need. we grow old.
why does she not appear
before us before we die?
still and still, he says
over and over, be mine.

VALENTINE 1975

i gave her a wand,
a staff of life,
a staff of light,
with bands of all
the colors running
down it, lotus at
the head, a wand
with which to magic.
she disappeared,

she disappeared,
the wand remains.
i gave her a
footstool too, so
she could rest her
feet. she ran. the
footstool is here.
the gifts given, and
the gifts left behind.
valentine day and
no presents left.
no presence left.
once more then into
the breach. learning
to take the armor off.
dan cupid are you
still aiming? valentine's
day i await you open-
handed empty-handed open-
mouthed exposed baring
my heart once again.

CULTURAL OPPRESSION

spring: the old
man watching young
girls playing
ball. odysseus
protect you old man
you will be turned
into a pig.

3/20/72

at 7:22 this
am my five
year old was
lacing up
his shoes, my
little one was
chewing on
his teether, my
wife was peeing,
i watched the
news on tv,
which is how
i found that
spring had sprung
bringing visions
of croci daff-
odillioes and
tulips blooming.
it was twenty-
eight degrees, a
schoolday, and
the sun just
angled round the
corner of the
building hitting
square against
the far side
of the courtyard
out my window.

SPRING AND SOME

the woman coming toward me
wears a red cape. she smiles
she likes my red hat and
she says so. the temperature
is dropping rapidly, the wind
is rising. they had predicted
rain and possibly snow; i
had not believed them. still
my red hat threatens to
blow away and her red cape
swirls about her. she says
i like your red hat, i smile
and say i like your red cape.
spring is coming by the
calendar, a red letter day,
but this day the temperature
drops, the wind blows up,
rain and possibly snow loom,
and we pass. red hat. red cape.

23 MARCH

art, zat strain
means a daft
i do
        in which
tzara married
irrevocably us
and his dada
manifesto

HYACINTHUS
an april fool

hi, a
shy cunt. hunt
shy i, a. c.
ah, tushy inc.
such tiny ah.
uh, i shy, can't.

3 APRIL 1972

according to the an-
archist calendar on
my bathroom wall, just
90 years ago today
that dirty little coward
he shot mr howard and
laid jesse james in
his grave, oh lord!

was it so short a time?
i thought it was an
age and a half – not
a day somebody i
might have known might
have seen or heard
the sound of, robert
ford's pistol cracking
in the quiet afternoon,
jesse on a chair, as
he straightened out
that picture on the
wall, the world crumbling
over and over, the
anarchist calendar is
quite correct to print
this significant date.

FOR THE ANNUAL READING
9 may 1975

the cherry trees
finally abloom.
we have waited
so long for them
this year. each
year we wait a little
longer, and yet they
do come, their
fierce blossoming
in the gentle weather.

and i have told
you yes and yes
though you will not
believe me, so much
depends upon the
weather, how we
see each day. the
blossoming depends
upon that weather,
why not us?
                so,
finally it is here.
now we are opened
too. exposed, now
we can wait for
new awakenings,
for revelations,
now, yes, we wait
for intimacies.
we are ready. the
cherry trees become
our flag. we move
ahead, into it all.

THE ANNIVERSARY OF ONE DEATH
THE DATE OF ANOTHER, 7/22

JOHN DILLINGER

thirty-eight years ago to
day she put the finger on
you and the man shot you
down
          both dick tracy's
crimestoppers and the
anarchist calendar agree:
your death occurred on
this date
          it was hot
in chicago on that day
and you had gone to
the movies to escape
the heat
          john-john did
your mother ever call
you that cuddling your
head to her bosom there
in the middle of america

CHI-CHI

a giant panda the
chinese sold you out
the british displayed
you in a zoo
          they gave
you a russian lover
and he tried twice
and twice you rejected
him
          the americans
wouldn't let you in
there was a cold war

your name meant
mischievous little girl
in chinese
                    where
are the high places
the cool winds
the tender bamboo
of that birthplace

you who went to
your grave untouched
as emily dickinson

only life violated
either one of you

A THANKSGIVING GRACE

for that we eat
while we argue about feeding others
for that we live
while killing others
for that we prosper
while robbing others
for that we sing
while silencing others
for that we are ourselves
while making others be us too
for that we find love
while hating others
for that we learn
while we refuse to learn

he said:
"if we do not count this blessed
let us change our religion"

A DIFFICULT GRACE
for the children, thanksgiving 1974

that there is food. where?
that mother earth keeps us. where?
that father sky guards us. where?
that we pay our thanks to
mother earth and father sky. who?
what? when? where? why?
that there is honesty and decency. where?
that evil is defeated. huh?
that evil is losing ground. huh?
that we are getting better. huh?
that there is love.
                    there is love.
that there is enough love for all of us.
        is there enough love for all of us?
that the world is good. what is the world?
that in the touch of the world,
in the turn of the world,
is all the food we need.

GRACE

over the river
through the trees
grandmother's house

old and wise
she feeds us
we eat at her table

when we die
we will live there
forever

we are well fed
in her house
beside her

as we are not
in our own
very often

and the beds are soft
to sleep in there
in her house

for which we give thanks
and for this journey
we must keep taking
over the river
through trees
to her house

we give thanks
she has set a table
before us

THE NEW YEAR

signs and portents
omens
bodings
good and bad beginnings

it's january second

the leather-bound
slim-line
pocket diary
is still up-to-date

i have entered and attended
and then crossed out as done
everything

i have gone to the party
i have greeted the anival of friends
i have read at the church
i have spent 6.35 on a business lunch
and entered an address to be carried
into the new address book

there are things to do
as far ahead as january 17th
and this very friday i have lunch with vmc
it is clear i am entering something
is it the new year?
                i hope so
a woman smiled at me in the street today
which hasn't happened since 1972

on the other hand the butcher was closed
on wednesday instead of monday
and paul knows the lady who smiled at me
and he says she is crazy

the world remains but then so do i

and the sun which rose this morning
showed that world to me
                      i hug
the ground to make my tour

i keep up-to-date at least this far
and the year is two days old

THE BIRTHRIGHT

there is a corollary
in astrology that tells us
it's not only the time
of our birth but place as well
that determines houses
we are born to

the astrologer speaks
while i bemoan the fame
i'm lacking
                tells me
my sun needs moving
into the tenth house
since that controls such things

i run to the atlas
and discover that tenth house
holds novaya zemla
workuta perm sverdlovsk
omsk karaganda tashkent
karachi the long sweep
of the indian ocean
the seychelles the maldives
mauritius la reunion and down
at the very bottom of the map
heard island sitting on
the kerguelen-gaussberg ridge

what a choice it is
russian pakistani penguin
what a way to be famous
in our time

my father would not be able
to commute from such far places
my mother couldn't seek
the foods she knew i needed

suppose the boys i'd run with
or the girls so nubile twelve
or even younger in such places

suppose the clothes or language
i would have to deal with

suppose what my stars might lack
in any of those places
and the poems i'd write or
never would have written

suppose fame for a lonely figure
dancing in siberian snowscapes

if it had only been tahiti
or kabul i would have moved
even ulan bator to which it
comes so close
                the fault is
not in our stars but in ourselves
where we were born so far

IF THERE WAS SENSE

to get there you would
have to come up the
missouri into the white,
or coming from the
west, cross the badlands.
from the south the
sand hills would
block you, you would
have to work to get
there. i sit here

writing, thinking
of where i should be
if there was sense,
thinking of all the
provisional brigades
silent, unmoving,
wondering where they
are, where we are.
thinking of the land
lost, the country
lost, the power lost
because no one moves.

if there were sense the
brigades would be forming,
the long columns would
stream toward wounded
knee. if there were
sense the passes would
clog with us, the
prairies would shake
with us, long files
would come riding up
from the south
carrying the deserts
with them.
               quakers
ready to lie down,
abolitionists risen
and fierce, lord
grizzly and the
mountain men, the
woodstock kids,
the angels even,
king's people, malcolm's,
black moslems, hanufi,
jews, irish, italians,
chinese, even the

buckleys screaming
for freedom. great
columns of smoke on
the horizon by day,
great plumes of dust
rising, great pillars
of fire by night. this
is a picture i could see
if there were sense.

if there were sense
i could hear
a gigantic shout: give
it to them, whatever
they want. give it
back. give it back.
let them have it, they
can do no worse. a
great irrational shout:
give them south dakota,
give them the black hills
and the great plains,
the prairies, taos,
blue lake, the mountains,
the father of rivers, the
woodlands, give them
manhattan, long island,
terre haute, the high land.
give them the thousand
lakes and the thousand
islands, give them
okefenokee and the great
dismal swamp, give them
their land. they can do
no worse. give them their
hostages against fate, their
lives against death, give them
give them give them give them.

MAN AND BOY

i was born
came out of my mother
nursed
lay in my crib
grew grew grew
talked and then walked
became a boy
went to school
learned lusted did
made sons
earned my keep
got tired
slept
worked some more
kept writing

suddenly
my oldest son
is living in his own house
shares it with a woman

and somewhere in kansas
a mother
is thinking over
the same chain
in respect to herself
and her beautiful daughter
i hope she's as happy
as i am
as renewed

i hope she's not
worried about aging

we could meet
to talk
it over

THE RE-ORGANIZATION

sorting
ordering it
what will we not find

letters bills receipts
answers unmailed or
not yet written
notices of ours and
everybody's work
advertisements and even poems

now each slides
into its own folder

if this one
had been answered
would i not now be teaching
in iowa and married
making steaks outdoors

if this one had not
been answered would i not
now be teaching in iowa married etcetera

each slides into its folder

the desk is clear and soon
the table also will be clear
and nothing will pile up from now on
and i will have
a flat red 'in' box and
a flat blue 'out' box so that
matters will be taken care of
and the bills also will be paid on time

and then i will write all the poems

SERVING NOTICE

i will not be
that single daddy
my friend had
roasting a leg of lamb
every sunday
slicing neat slices
through the week

these kids
will eat differently
every night

their clothes will fit
and not be put up with

and they will wear
their hats and rubbers

and in my bed
i'll dream whatever dreams
are necessary

and i'll curl those bodies
i can or want to
around my body

and i'll take the necessary time
and i will not make
leg of lamb each sunday
slicing slices through the week

CELEBRATING THE PEACE
9–15 may 1975

if you celebrate the end
of a war you are celebrating
that war.
        go home my
townspeople into your own houses
that is where peace begins.
              the war is starting
what speeches will you make
or hear that have not been
made or heard by you before?
            the war is starting again
in what way by gathering
to reconstruct air that was before?
how by gamboling before the orators
on sunny days to make a peace?
           the war never ended
you are gloating you are waving
flags in triumph.
        no god no master
the flags said in paterson so
long ago the silk strike the
only flag i wish to see no
wars no governments no states
they take umbrage like a human being.
          the war goes on forever
forget the dead people, forget
limbs piled in earlier bloody
wars, forget blasted innards, eyes
seared, leaves gone, earth scorched—
yes we did that too—forget
homeless people, peopleless houses,
forget helicopters falling in the water,
forget the gold that weighs those choppers down.
          the war is over but a ship has been
          captured by them and retaken by us
          and the choppers have landed the marines

no rhetoric will make it as it was.
the nature of peace changes by the war before.
dead grandparents would not recognize this peace.
and theirs would not recognize the peace they knew.
so many wars.
                there is no peace
if you must celebrate it. parade parade
march your banners and your selves you
are victors you have triumphed over
other people you have won. what? you
have won what? peace is the absence
of a triumph it is quiet singing in
your house and bed it is turning to
your own concerns and pleasures.
                        there is heavy small arms opposition
                        the enemy has released their captives
stop celebrating. *celeber* : frequented
or populous. wars. occasions of wars.
they are frequented, populous, the
people stream one way or the other
under orders or because of fear. peace
comes from *pactum*, a bargain, a bargain
made that we shall be left alone.
                        several choppers were downed in the assault
                        the ship has been returned
                        the men are safe
                        the marines are still engaged
let us lay down this burden down by
the riverside, let us feel peace
in our hearts and minds let us have
no more celebrations that celebrate
what we have beaten lest we forget
what it was was won and we become
conquerors and strut as certainly
as jack boots in another place.
                        the fighting goes on
                        the war goes on

crow triumph. peace cannot ever win.
destroy the word to save it. we
have heard that before.
                              there is no peace
build such a chain of people
you will not need to celebrate
you will not need these gatherings
except for the work of hands. these
other works will destroy us every time.
do not go to the party. do not
celebrate the end of war you
celebrate the war

                              there is never any peace
                              there will never be peace
                              the war goes on
                              the marines are landing
                              we don't take shit from anyone
                              we'll show them
                              peace is not a victory but a natural state
                              do not celebrate the end of war
                              nobody wins

AT FIFTY: A POEM

Loving means not letting immediacy wither
under the omnipresent weight of mediation and economics,
and in such fidelity it becomes itself mediated,
as a stubborn counterpressure.

He alone loves who has the strength
to hold fast to love . . . .

It is the test of feeling
whether it goes beyond feeling through permanence . . . .

The love which in the guise of unreflecting spontaneity,
and proud of its alleged integrity,
relies exclusively on what it takes to be
the voice of the heart, and runs away as soon as
it no longer thinks it can hear that voice,
is in this supreme independence precisely the tool of society . . . .

The fidelity exacted by society is a means of unfreedom,
but only through fidelity can freedom
achieve insubordination to society's command.

from *Minima Moralia*/Theodor Adorno

I

necessarily
the goddess is
unattainable
　　nympholepsy
　　that rapture attained
　　straining for the
　　unattainable
and the stroking
touches only surface

yet it causes her
to rise near those surfaces

the evidence is in
the sounds

II

written:
i felt desire
but wanted love

to another:
which is not to say
i won't try to
seduce you archaic
notion to make us
laugh together

to another:
a partly empty bed
awaits you
          sadly
this brought her here

to another:
no! no! no! no! no!
to another:
yes and yes and yes

III

waking middle night
walking the hall
smell of pine-sol
one smell and back now
shades of proust
whirling back
eight years old
annie the cleaning lady
across from me at lunch

soup sucked straight up
from saucer poured from bowl

clothes layer on layer
smell slightly stale and sour
smell of cleaning cleaning

old fat ugly an anomaly
this woman spends her life
cleaning other people's houses

cooled the soup in the saucer
and her coffee also

then swung back further
three or four years old
sharing the room with
anna the young strong
depression girl hired
to help sick mother
tend little boy and house
me and anna at the church
at mount st vincent feeding
the goldfish in the pool
outside it then inside
curled in corner of
a pew while anna prayed
and made confession

one night in bed but not asleep
watched anna slide from dress
stand in slip readying to go out
first woman i saw undressed
natural my eve my astarte

anna young going out
with bill the cop she married
and smelled different
and was desirable and formed
my image of a woman

IV

the blouse was
sequined it
caught the hand

anything for
beauty she said

reaching through
the neck fondled
her breast nipples
filled my hand
i love them

i think you love
women she said

may just have been
right or perhaps
it is only nipples

V

i did ask if
you'd marry me
the first time
we met but that
was for ulterior
motives the things
you owned and had
in storage three
hand presses and
a lot of type
unable to ask
for heavier things
thinking you were
already incumbered

in response to
my query about
unincumbered
the editor said
perhaps it isn't
le mot juste
for referring to
the state of being
unmarried
but your letter says
you are unincumbered

so marry me

VI

oh rachel
            your
wide shoulders
                  your
small breasts surprised
me so as the
blouse fell from
your back

VII

not only beautiful
but also willing in addition
to read two year's worth
of an obscure trade journal
to find me a copy
of an early publication
a note on why j and u
appear as they do
in the type case
not to mention the
alphabet and did
find it even though
my name was not used

perception perception
to know me so well
before knowing me
and when i was young
as you and also
did not know me

VIII

a lot of body hair
has gone
            rubbed off
by furies i suppose

hundreds of them
all these years

IX

the heat rises
in us also

X

one would-be customer
complained to the local precinct
about his black eye
broken nose missing teeth

told police he went to the mansion
for oral sex went into
the wrong room and was beaten

XI

were you really
a model once

i was featured
in a movie

XII

a fool always a fool
for young women
                    when
young a young fool

now a middle-aged and
soon to be an old one

before they had
to be crazy and young
now they need be young only

and where before
they said it was because
i was a poet
              now it's because
they have this hang-up see
about older men

XIII

she was perfect still
though twenty years
later
        and she undressed
so quickly yes too
quickly
            perfect
she undressed

XIV

at last i understand
the young
              are for
the young

you will never warm
these bones with
that flesh
          that flesh
will warm bones
that need no warming

oh you will come
because i need never
because you want

also i will watch
as he watches
you and see his
face light as
mine stays dark

at last i
understand this

XV

cleanliness is next
to godliness especially
this once in twenty-eight
years easter and pesach
coincide and so
i do my laundry

there is a note
on the bulletin board

whoever has my blue genes
please return them

> To arrive at the simplest truth . . . .
> requires years of contemplation.
> Not activity.
> Not reasoning.
> Not calculating.
> Not busy behavior of any kind.
> Not reading.
> Not talking.
> Not making an effort.
> Not thinking.
> Simply bearing in mind what it is one needs to know.

from *Laws of Form* /G Spencer Brown

I

you smell good she
said like in eighth grade

followed by stories
of her grandpa
and the skunks

how to take that

II

rain
        breasts
            new pink dress
allowed only the first i
imagine april in your letter

III

strange winter with
spring before
groundhog day and

warm rain then
and dropping tonight
and back to winter

but he will not
see his shadow while
it rains

and spring will come
quickly then

time to oil up
the baseball glove
and get the arm
back in shape

IV

in the seat
of a car
like teenagers

grandson asleep
in the house
twelve feet away
dreaming of mother's
nipples and milk
sweet and warm

what were we
dreaming of

V

spent the night
talking who is
your favorite writer
deja vu of thirty
years ago and not since

good list for prose
but the poets left
something to be desired

which was the point
to leave something
to be desired ah

to bed alone both poets
both desiring both
waiting for it yet

VI

we open like flowers
and then we discover
why the rose has thorns

VII

trying to explain
to a blonde who lives
with somebody else
and a waitress
i hardly know
they both look summery
which they take to mean
they are unclothed

of course but to explain
i can see breasts any time
but shoulders bared
in the streets and
in public restaurants
only in summer and
i like it summery

they think i want their bodies
and don't know how it eases me
simply to see their shoulders

the last b'rucha of
the two hundred and sixteen
says thanks for the making
of beauty on this earth

VIII

at my age she said i
am tired of men who are
still working out their
anger against mother

i said let it
serve notice

IX

summers are
full of love
for us

winters
we are old men

X

some women having let
their body hair grow
are then disturbed to find
their husbands find it erotic
when that was not the point

XI

a postcard from nice
la promenade des anglais
obviously a french joke
since les anglais
don't go bare-breasted
yet inset bare-breasted

maiden large straw hat
shading her eyes and
one hand holding it
brown nipples atilt

dear joel it's true
on every beach
you never know
where to look
not good form
to be caught gaping
unfortunately
what we've always
known is true
the ideal tits
are in our heads
but then one set
comes by and

and he is a painter
and he ought to know

XII

have stick will
travel says
the journeyman printer
knowing the journey
really means working
day by day you
don't own the shop
and stay there
all the days

it's not taking
a trip not
necessarily moving
in so cumbered
is a good word
angel woman
alas in chicago

while i do
my day's work
un incumbered here
in new york

XIII

it is two days since
the lady said i am
comfortable but cautious
as i kissed her full
soft cold lips to
no response and it is
three days since the
lady couldn't dance
because of sciatica
and four days past
the lady who didn't
answer her phone

XIV

three years later
live cigar in my hand
she asked are you
still smoking

inhaled and said
no but i moved
the catbox

now it doesn't
stink up the kitchen
it wouldn't offend
you any more

the same round
breasts and face
three years later

but like miss crab
said to mr lobster
after learning
to walk frontwards

would you please
get out of my way

XV

aphrodite
she says last night
she read my words
while rude boys called

for meat she said
they want just meat
to ease themselves
and not her self

o she is wrong
beautiful one
they want only
you
    i also

and sometimes meat
body calling
other bodies

sometimes as more

yes
    love us all
as we love you
or let us be
needless
       alone

the more laws and restrictions
the poorer the people

the sharper the weapons
the more trouble

the more ingenious and clever
the more strange things happen

the more rules and regulations
the more thieves and robbers . . . .

from *The Way and The Power*/Lao Tse

I

xeng-li the name
means success the sex
not definitely known
but thought to be male
the child of pe-pe and yin-yin
born in a zoo in mexico city

an international storm the
director of the washington
zoo mexico has lucked out
completely their pandas are young
and just barely sexually mature
and everything must have happened
at just the right time
and they must have liked each other

it is hard to find compatible pandas

II

to you i was always an enemy
you were always an enemy to me

but they look at us
and see no difference
we are all enemies to them

and they to us of course

III

despite my
own labors
and the kids
there was
a mouse in
nat's waste
basket a
triumph again
of nature
over art

IV

seeking seeking a new discipline
on which to base their careers
two psychiatrists look at the artwork

a sculpture two thousand years old
from the shaft tombs of western mexico
shows a woman just after giving birth

they say she is suffering from
classic post-partum depression

we know from history later on
aztec midwives tried to stop these blues
by assuring new mothers they'd behaved
like the eagle and the tiger
and had won a real battle
just like the bravest soldiers

in four other figures they say they see
cases of true or clinical depression
as distinguished from simple grief or madness
and presumably also post-partum depression

and another is taciturn gloomy despondent
which is yet another image of the same they say

a thousand years later late classic maya
shows them an old woman biting her nails
and they say this typifies yet another
state of agitated depression which often
accompanies advancing age even today i say
while another elderly man from this period
has a bland expression drooping lip
and is presumed silent which they say
are also characteristics of ditto
and in fact to them the figure's stare
recalls galen's description of
the melancholic state dread and desire
death both at the same time

galen also lived a long time ago
but not as long ago as some old people
although longer ago than the shrinkers

anyhow all these old statues cause them
to conclude these peoples recognized
dementia and other psychoses and there
is of course ample proof that the aztecs
conferred with the spanish about at least two
forms of depression after losing to them

the question is mostly are all
psychiatrists fools or only these
of course our ancestors bit their
nails at walls and stayed
silent impressed by the act of

giving birth to another or the
equally impressive act of aging

they too got depressed and galen too

and god knows i do reading
these tedious theories forced
into life to bolster their jobs and
stop their fingernail biting which
led them into psychiatry in the
first place
                    better to stare at walls
but they'll never discover that

V

weeds are a purely
arbitrary designation
saying hey you you're
a weed you're not
a flower as if they were
some separate species

i prefer the german
way of looking at it
unkraut no cabbage

if you can't eat it
and you can't paint
it then fuck it and
if you can't even do
that you might as
well salute it the
gi's used to say

VI

seven-thirty in the morning
couple in shiny english boots

whipcord jodhpurs riding caps
blue broadcloth shirts whips
walking down hudson there
are no stables that way

VII

the vegetarian piranha
live on fruits and seeds

large molars and muscled jaws
let them crack hard nuts
in the flood plains of brazil
among the watery forests

the fish then shit the seeds
and the trees are born again

in rapid succession you'll hear
a pop when the pods explode to
scatter the seeds and a plop
when a seed hits the water and
a gulp when the fish swallows it

if you cut down the trees
you're bound to decrease the catch

VIII

they set up headquarters
registered the prospectors
declared the site closed
to any others
vaccinated the colony
against yellow fever and meningitis
banned women and alcohol
announced that anyone
firing a weapon
would be expelled

set up a loudspeaker
to play country music
during off hours
and the national anthem
at morning and evening
flag raising and lowering

each night soft-core
pornographic films
are shown on the airstrip

IX

the soviets have opened war
on the villages of afghanistan
students businessmen professionals
commute to battle next
to moslem holy warriors

X

the leader of the basques
fighting for autonomy
says no political entity
can live without a
coercive apparatus

i am reading this
two days after the anniversary
of the fall of the bastille

presumably that coercive apparatus
is what we have all been fighting for

XI

surely in buffalo
there's one bar

where they want us
to come and sit
and talk all night
just a bar to talk

XII

eleven years ago
i stopped making love
to watch cleon jones
put the team ahead
in a crucial game

stopped the act of love
to watch baseball
on television
a ballclub in
a pennant race

not important except
to remember committing
this act life vs art
art vs art culture vs
the individual whatever

eleven years later
there is always something
embarassing to remember
something we did that was
shameful ridiculous and
shameful something
to wish undone

but that marriage is gone
and the team won the pennant

XIII

and here's your checklist
for mother's day

heinz beans
del monte tomato sauce
ronzoni spaghetti
aqua-fresh toothpaste
minute maid orange juice
dellwood low fat milk
temtee whipped cream cheese
pepsi cola
lipman chickens
boneless london broil
boneless turkey cutlets
ground chuck
fresh salads
lean boiled deli ham

most stores open sunday

XIV

each day
is one day gone
and you should not
understand this

you are not fifty

XV

devil kissed me

saw cathedral
                    but in plan

not real

Our life today is poisoned to the root. Man has ousted the beasts and trees, has poisoned the air, and filled up the open spaces. Worse things may happen. That melancholy and industrious animal—man—may discover new forces and harness them to his chariot. Some such danger is in the air. The result will be a great abundance—of human beings! Every square yard will be occupied by a man. Who will be able then to cure us of the lack of air and space? The mere thought of it suffocates me.

But it is not only that, not only that. Every effort to procure health is in vain. Health can only belong to the beasts, whose sole idea of progress is in their own bodies . . . spectacled man invents instruments outside his body, and if there was any health or nobility in the inventor there is none in the user. Implements are bought or sold or stolen, and man goes on getting weaker and more cunning. It is natural that his cunning should increase in proportion to his weakness. The earliest implements only added to the length of his arm, and could not be employed except by the exercise of his own strength. But a machine bears no relationship to the body. The machine creates disease because it denies what has been the law of creation throughout the ages. The law of the strongest disappeared, and we have abandoned natural selection. We need something more than psychoanalysis to help us.

Under the law of the greatest number of machines, disease will prosper and the diseased will grow ever more numerous.

Perhaps some incredible disaster produced by machines will lead us back to health.

When all the poison gases are exhausted, a man, made like all other men of flesh and blood, will in the quiet of his room invent an explosive of such potency that all the explosives in existence will seem like harmless toys beside it. And another man, made in his image, and in the image of all the rest, but a little weaker than them, will steal that explosive and crawl to the center of the earth with it, and place it just where he calculates it would have the maximum effect. There will be a tremendous explosion, but no one will hear it and the earth will return to its nebulous state and go wandering through the sky, free at last from parasities and disease.

from *Confessions of Zeno*/Italo Svevo

I

bewildered in the
morning heat
i take an apricot
i take a plum

though they taste
good to me only
the first bite
is accurate in
what we expect

finally they cloy
too much or not
enough of what
we eternally desire

nothing is ever
perfect in this world

one bite is perfect
still it leads
to another

II

in albuquerque
they want bridges
over the rio grande
to save time

they will wreck
the centuries old
irrigation system

they want
even more cars
they will block
the whooping cranes

who fly over
they are already
blanketed by
pollution every winter

but rush hour
has worsened

the fight is
over technicalities

at the northern tip
of the unbridged stretch
is one of the last stands
of primitive cottonwoods

the last stand

III

seeing the woman
corner of bleecker and bank
paper in hand blank look
asking for help

where are you going

whither goest thou

wanted west broadway
castelli gallery
you're a far piece
she was just that
since she was swedish

it's a walk if you don't mind
she smiled no are you maybe
walking also that way
no i go this but

if you stay on bleecker
long enough you'll

crazy walking by interjected
go straight to hell
you know i said
he's right follow bleecker
down to la guardia
go right past houston
you'll get there
gallery or hell

left her smiling swedish

IV

amenophis III
akhenaten
smenkhkare
and tutankhamen
's mummy cases
show them with
female breasts

the doctor says
these were real
the result of
hereditary
pseudohermaphroditism
so common in families
with a long history of incest

pharaohs of the eighteenth dynasty
commonly married their sisters
daughters and other close relatives

and oedipus as we know
across the mediterranean
went blind because
he was a bad mother fucker

V

the topic sentence says
by any rational calculation
the potential benefits
vastly outweigh potential costs

the first major point is
suppose one or more
great oil spills blight the region

it is answered that
the economic loss would be great
but not greater than the losses
from the eruption of mt st helens
or the droughts that strike
the grain belt every decade or two

the second major point is
the ecological damage
would also be terrible

it is answered that it would not be
more terrible than the damage
inflicted on the deserts of the southwest
by poor land-use planning

the third major point states that
those who prefer to go slow
note that the oil would not disappear
if it were left in place for another decade

and this is answered that
unfortunately the timing of the flow
could be critical to economic stability

so in summing up it says
every effort should be made
to exploit the alaskan oil reserve

with minimal environmental damage
but whatever the valid hesitations
they should not be allowed
to cloud our economic future

to which the teacher comments that the
rhyme interjected into the last
clause of allowed and cloud is
distracting and unfortunate
and that our economic future has
been clouded anyway since the
industrial revolution began
since man began
to eat himself

VI

he rings the bell
for his friend
at five of eight
this morning
his towel and
bathing suit
slung over shoulder

it is the fourth hot day

she comes by and tells me
harry is dead

she wants to discuss
the fact that he kept
taking himself out
of the hospital
wouldn't stay in
and now is dead

she says he was
too young to die

all people die too young
but could a hospital
have helped him

but i cannot debate this now
since these kids are ready
and i must pay attention
to their needs

always when someone dies
there are kids eight and ten
needing attention

even when homer and chaucer died
and when i die also

so we go downstairs
to meet the bus
so then they can swim
this hot day

while harry's grave waits
at another end of the city

VII

wrestled to the ground
like jacob or the angel
hogtied by six presby
terian ministers all
i wanted was my damned
breakfast they were
visiting the college
for a one-day program
in handling stress i
figured they wanted
to see how much they
could put me under

while we talked
about god and secular
humanism i
took to staring out
the windows and saw
how the lake'd been
lowered for winter
so the weeds would
die the larvae too
to benefit next
summer's season
it was a man-made
lake in which now
the stumps and all
the bric-a-brac
showed with water
only toe-deep

i said well at
least this here's
a great place now for
walking on the waters

and finished off my
breakfast in the peace
that passeth understanding

VIII

teachers dissatisfied
world fertility in
rapid decline what
are those lights
on the moon

IX

belltower's computer
tells seasons

i see orion
high in night sky

X

ciba-geigy corp

glens falls

general electric

hudson falls

chase bag company
general electric

fort edward

scott paper company

schuylerville
stillwater
mechanicville

general electric
park guilderland sewage treatment plant

troy

al tech specialty steel corporation
bendix corporation
ford motor company

albany north wastewater treatment plant
rensselaer county sewer district

rensselaer

chemical leaman tank lines
ashland chemical company

albany

albany south wastewater treatment plant
albany steam station
consolidated rail corporation
general electric
lion brand corporation

catskill

alpha portland cement
dutchess metal finishes

kingston

hercules incorporated
culligan water conditioning
western publishing
ibm

poughkeepsie

poughkeepsie water treatment plant
central hudson gas and electric
new york trap rock
three star anodizing
ibm

beacon

montgomery worsted mills

newburgh

texaco
tuck industries
marathon battery
majestic weaving company incorporated
consolidated edison

peekskill

state power authority
orange and ruckland utilities
u s gypsum
lightron corporation
orange and rockland utilities

tarrytown

federal paper board
glenshaw glass
anaconda wire and cable division
phelps dodge wire and cable company
town of west new york
city of new york
city of hoboken
jersey city sewage authority

jersey city
newark

new york city

and the 'american
rhine' flows thus
unbroken to the sea

thalassa! thalassa!

XI

you can write anything
someone will listen and applaud
but to write something
and to listen yourself
and still applaud

XII

or to arrive at a place
and say this is the place
that kills

of course the people
but the place also

and to wake there alone

XIII

brewing plant compounds
in the kitchen
is not everyone's
cup of tea

many american and
european women
would rather take a pill
because it seems
more scientific

they are trying
to isolate
the secret ingredient
of this herbal
birth control
so it can be
duplicated in
the laboratory

the beauty
is its simplicity

it is common
and found in many
parts of the world

all a woman has to do
is sip the bitter
herbal tea the morning
after sex and her
worries will be over

but a pill seems
more scientific

but they will be
silent until the
experiments are
completed

women will be able
to grow and gather it
and make their tea

but a pill seems
more scientific

of course a needle would
be even more so
but a pill is the
middle road no

and mum is the word
and mom is a word too
and so is apple pie
with the bitter tea

every morning when
the experiments
are complete

XIV

mao sd
there is no
occident

XV

others have said it
and i repeat i repeat

Pain and love—the whole of life, in short — cannot be looked
on as a disease just because they make us suffer.

—from *Confessions of Zeno*/Italo Svevo

DEL QUIEN LO TOMÓ :: A SUITE

this
is an homage

for paul blackburn
and for him that gave it

ADORNMENT OF BODY POEM

once, younger, with
a woman i loved, i
made her body naked,
took out her jewelry,
dressed her in all of it.
i draped eighteen
necklaces around her neck,
the longer, heavier ones,
the ones with stones or
pendants, all fell
between, around, on top
of her breasts.   the
smaller ones circled
her naked neck.   as
many earrings as i
could fit i put on
her ears, i loaded both
her arms with bracelets.
a brooch was balanced
in her navel.   i took
each piece off slowly,
both of us much aroused.

some years later, with
a different woman that
i loved, i made her
naked, took out her jewelry,
tied her in it as
best i could, binding
necklaces around her
breasts, her thighs, i
clipped the earrings
on her nipples, on
the lips of her cunt,
and then i ate her,
both of us much aroused.

now it is even later.
i watch you clothed.
i hold you, then
i kiss you. i take
your clothes off slowly.
you are in a bigger rush
than i am. i hold you
naked. we fuck,
both of us much aroused.

THE JANE ST POEM

1

as i
walked along
the street in

the morning light
first the right
leg so

carefully
then the left
stepped square

into a dream of
your sweetest
honeypot

2

walking home at
5 am summer morning
and domes of churches
golden now, coffee
starting in the urn,

i walk by quickly,
avoiding that and
talk, it is peaceful
in the street, it was
noisy inside me
in your arms.

3

and now another
time walking
home 6:30 summer
morning an old man
no majesty still
asleep on park bench
heaped a pile of
papers a used sermon
no dog to keep
him warm, it is
summer.
          young again
laughing i walk home.

4

working off a body
of unshared experiences
—how will we ever know?—
the images collect and
juxtapose, in secret.
which is to say that
forty-five is in that sense
different from twenty-five
which is different again from twenty.
and green glass is in
the gutter, though this gutter
is macadamized.   still
the green glass glitters.
it is early sunlight

catching it, near the
old folks home.

and last night i
thought a square of
lighted window pane
in the corner was
the dawn beginning.
it was four-fifteen
and there was time.

5

all this is for you.
even lovers running
giggling down the street
while i walk to meet you
back straight and head
held high.   you don't see
the way i walk to meet you
with the street sharper
in my eyes until i see
the way i ought to
all the time.   it is
for you even on other
nights we only touch or kiss
or even when i don't
see you at all.   it is
seeing differently
and i want to tell you.

AUTUMN

the weather
moving
one side of the continent
to the other

in the park
one relaxed arm
drapes easily
over her friend's arm

movement
touch
how they work

all i know
the body
the poem

THE GHOST LOVER

this poem
is for
theresa

real

the image
won't disappear

it isn't fair
to call your
breast an image

i know that

still this image
won't go away

i am alone
in my bed now
still your body
presses itself
against me

your breast round
in my hand as
we press i press
and fondle it
wonderingly as
i have always done
not understanding
breasts or women

ghost lover now
in my bed
when i had supposed
i was happy
and suppose i am
regardless

but you are here

your breast was larger
than i'd imagined
when i hugged you
the first time

the time we met
after a long time
a long time after
we had eyed each other
for weeks knowing
eventually
we would hug
and press against
each other some time

so we met again
not having seen
each other
in a year or more
a year in which
to grow thought
and desire both
and we grew them

we hugged each other
then you later than
you'd thought to be
so there was that
pressure too
of time upon us
and you ran toward me
into my arms
surprising me
and yourself also
i thought then
and know now
with the intensity

but i had hoped
for just that
intensity as
all potential

lovers will
in their dreams
dreaming the
desired one
desires us

your breasts
pressed against me
in that meeting
larger than i thought
from hours of
my eyes undressing
you while we
had talked before

later in my bed
freed they were
larger still

tonight alone here
your breast round
presses on my hand

this is a dream
yet i place my hand
upon your venus-mount

venus-mount
is also the name
of the fleshy part
between thumb and
palm of hand
which when squeezed
by thumb held up
and in toward palm
and not turned over
mounds and is used
to tell capacity
for love and passion

if it is firm
you are passionate
if full you are full
of loving feelings

if it is both
the palm reader says
you are the perfect lover

to be full of loving
is not always the same
as being passionate
we have learned

and venus-mount
to mount venus
that need rides me
always always

psyche never
the problem
always venus
aphrodite
ishtar astarte
that goddess
larger than
i'd expected ever

in any event
fleshy mound in which
you are buried
or any woman
and in which
i bury myself
from time to time

loving that joining
loving venus
sometimes loving you

now my hand on it
cradling it cupping

this flesh also
is firm and round

beneath it i find
your hole is wet
your hole takes
several fingers in
and makes sucking sounds

this is truth

though i am alone
in my bed tonight
and another woman
fills my thoughts
fills me too

my fingers deep in you
several of them
and you pressed
up against me
now my hand
moves from round breast
to bottom and enters
that hole also
and one finger
drives you there
then returns to breast

you move against me
with each touch
you are panting
you kiss me panting
it is rich
and satisfying

for me to feel
you panting as
you press against me

your vagina
sucks my fingers
and you come
with whimpers
around them

you spoke then
that first night
you begged me
not to enter you
you said you'd
been raped young
at thirteen
a man'd entered
you forcibly

so you beg me
not to enter you
while my hand is
still still on
your venus-mount
my fingers still
deep inside you

i nod assent
and your hands
go to stroking me

i surrender thoughts
of being inside you
and i come myself
to that warm hand
stroking and pulling

my hand still on
your breast now stroking
pulling feeling nipple
between my fingers
harder harder and below
my fingers still
inside you riding
to your rhythm
as you ride to mine

we spent four nights
sleeping this way

days we walked
museums together
moved by that which
surrounded us
and moved too by
what invaded us
filled with what
we had found ourselves

four nights and
i never entered
inside you
touched only surface
over and over
and somehow still
was satisfied

i believe you were too
with your hand on me
with my hand in you
stroking pulling
into release
each of us then

but why do you return

i am happy now
alone tonight still
there is a woman
real and loving
she wants me
as i want her

i dream of her also
but you intrude

you haunt me
the image won't go
breasts firm and large
you afraid of entry
not afraid of me
how else allow
fingers deep in you
afraid of entry
and me not willing
to force that entry
afraid to force
myself in you

we could never
have been happy
this way more
than four nights
i know that
hands on each other
in each other
kissing good lips
tongues touching
bodies touching
each deep in the other
and yet not

no we could not
have been very happy

so why do you
keep returning
and why does
this image remain

i cannot enter
your ghost hole
any more than the flesh
and do not want to

have done have done
leave me in peace

ii

i desire another
and she desires me

my lover's round breast
fills my hand

March–April 1982
New Hampshire

GENERATIONS

For My Family
1893–the present

and particularly
for the sons
not mentioned here
but in other places
and other poems
and for the son's son
who continues the line

. . . your sons and your daughters shall prophesy
your old men shall dream dreams
your young men shall see visions . . .

joel 2:28

CHILD

not to be able
to touch one's
mother not her
arm to lift her
what she did to
cut off touching
now not able
to lift her while
my brother does
he learned how to
touch from her
i did not

WHAT MY FATHER SAID

about words with unpronounced letters in them
silent like the "p" in swimming

how to go fishing with a can of peas and a baseball bat
open the can and sprinkle on the water
when the fish come up to take a pea
hit them over the head with the baseball bat

don't ask for too much
i have tried to get brown sauce on my meat for twenty years

if you are going into a partnership make sure you hate him
you will keep an eye on him all the time

if you want to be a garbage man
make sure you are the best garbage man there is

don't sleep with women of the street
that are dirty

the apple didn't fall far from the tree

MOTHER

i saw her sex
naked, pouched
grim as her lips
sunken her
teeth gone

her one eye
glazed open
her lost eye
sunken shut

her sex naked
barely haired
apparent

the nurse
businesslike
while i oh god
seeing it

naked and hairless

DEATH

nat fourteen said

she had a philosophy
of her own

wear your galoshes
dress warm
bears don't go to bars

but maybe
one day that

philosophy
will rule the
world

no one will catch cold
and no
bears will get
drunk

THE OLDEST

mother
was stone

teeth bit

sisters none
i longed

two wives
no longer

never daughters

now one
i flower

loving him
same mystery

we share that

SON

nat eleven

like
    a never ending road
    an eclipse
    a bad book
    morning t.v.
    a kid with no big brother
    a worn out ball point pen
    a slum
    me . . .

GROWING

six days into
the eleventh year
there are younger
there are older
there is nothing
i can say

truffaut keeps trying
at twenty-seven he
made the four hundred
blows to show how
bad twelve can be
and at forty-four
he made small change
to show how good

i see the same
burgeonings of
lust and love as
you sit staring
into skin magazines

when i say haven't
you seen your mother
naked and annie her
small breasts pointed
as we changed our
swimsuits that june
afternoon when you
were ten and saw
you look at me
as if i'm crazy
and i am

what have these
to do with your
dreams these real
women as i suppose
when the young boys
gathered in
the bush or caves
to dream their
fantasies and
jerk them off

as if to bridge
the generation gap
i say i'm still
doing just that
at forty-seven
as if that provided
some essential link

still truffaut tried
and failed he
didn't say it
not exactly
no one can

at thirteen fathers
can say to children
we are all the same

no one believes
it or should

RITUAL

this shawl, son,
this wrap, this
fringed garment
is your sign

you have come
of age
        you may
read the words
and live by them

you may approach
the book and read

you may carry
the words with you
as you in this shawl

it is of the desert
and it has covered us
everywhere
            we start
from nothing, from
the dry dust
            we grow
with the word
until we flower

flower well

YOUNGEST GRACE

lem seven

thank you for the food before us
thank you for the table before us
thank you for the friends next to us
thank you for this house
thank you for the trees
thank you for the bushes
thank you for everyone
thank you for thanksgiving

LIFE

i wish
there were rules
to give you

there used to be

my father gave them
to me even if
they didn't work

he lectured
day after day
how to behave
what to hope for
what to wear
what not to do

but those rules
have all gone now
and i no longer
know anything

still i will have
to find something
to let you sleep
each night out there

it's a hard road
you will need
some rules to last

i wish too
i could say
i love you
some other way
than just the words
but the words
will have to do
since we can't
hug any more
the same way
now that
you've grown big
but i hug you
anyway
with these words

and add
i'll have dinner
on the table
when you get back
tonight from
your first day
at work
            out there

TORAH

> and what doth the Lord
> require of thee
> but to do justly
> and to love mercy
> and to walk humbly
> with thy God
> > micah 6:8

it is such
a simple text
saying again
and again

fathers to sons
"he told me that
and i did not
listen"
> now
i listen and hear

it is not He
who has forsaken me

it is me who has
forsaken Him
and this simple
text
> again

NEW SPACES: POEMS 1975-1983

DRAWING FROM LIFE

STATEMENT TO THE CITIZENS

we are here, working,
hungering for bread.

you are there, living,
hungering.

           can there not
be commerce between us

THESE DAYS

all the young mothers
used to say
they didn't mind
the kids in the park
it was the other mommas
they had to talk to
being stuck there

the fathers said
they didn't mind
that so much
it was the kids

now i see the
bank street park
is filled with
poppas watching
babies crawl

the mommas stand
to the side talking

neither doing
what it wants
and maybe not
the babies either

TALKING

all of us
sit together
in the bar

some of us
are drinking

all of us
see the ghosts
before us

some of us
talk with them
and the rest
run to each other

we are talking
about him
whether with each other
or the ghosts

we are talking
about him
where he lies
alone on a bed
with ghosts
too alive
to bear

and there are always
more than enough
ghosts to talk to

all those voices
we carry within

those voices
that eat us up

lying alone on that bed
ghosts visit him

what they say
may be important
but we have to come out
come out of ourselves

there are conversations
with real people
waiting for us

CAMILLE OLDER

everything i have learned
is scratched into me
deeply as can be

i cough this morning
getting up
and it is 1951

where did dan go

why aren't we laughing

comparing the rasp
of our morning barks

why is this cough different

scaring me
heart into mouth

thinking of mother death
and her house

thinking of waking alone there
without friends

NATHANIEL'S VALENTINE

very beautiful picture for
my mom
                it is broken after *beau,*
ful, picture, and *my.* the m
in *my* is a w. opposite on a
blue field the figure sits.
the part below the waterline a
fish a boat? above facelike perhaps
a man. straight lines as in
buildings, the building we
live in. is this my son
forming? jung might say so.
the lettering runs on brown, the
two sheets neatly pasted together

to form a page in this book.

THE ANSWER NOT GIVEN

you worry about which clothes
to cover you in which situation

what is it i'm not allowed
to objectify having found
you beautiful all ways

the clothes or fit were not
what prompted the response

i cannot of course deny
that they gave me pleasure

yet you have presented yourself
as object to all the others
and i have responded differently
from the very beginning

i found you beautiful i've said
but then i did not understand

ONE DAY AT A TIME

he said that thursday said
it would be friday's friend

he said this because he was waiting
because on friday he would get
a belated christmas gift
and he had asked me
when friday would get here

i said it would get here
right after thursday

hooray for thursday he said
he said that thursday said
he would be friday's friend

i wish i could be that clear-headed
that relaxed about waiting

like being able to say
that the night before the night
we finally touch each other
is that night's friend

THIS WAS SOME SORT OF HAIKU

we lived together ten years
and i curled my fingers
in your brown hair
brushed it
even washed it for you

we meet in the park
you tell me smiling
not to laugh at you
but i notice nothing

one hour later
my new friend, curly-haired,
laughing while she does so
tells me about your haircut
tells me how strange it looks

THE MODERNIST

he said
study greek
and latin
if you want
to be a poet

he said
only the sounds
matter not
the meaning

those were the
first two lessons

then he stopped
coming to class

LEGEND

a cairn is
a marker of rocks
thrown up over
the hero's grave

or points the way

end or beginning
or both still
thing placed by path

not to know
what it stands for
since the knowing
just might stop us

to know only
that it stands
points down or out
and that we ought
to do something

i have erected
this cairn but
do not know yet
if i am buried here
or have moved on
leaving this sign
for who comes next

there may be
another ahead

NIGHT AND DAY

the man in the
picture looks down
from the wall over
the bed lent for
the night
            for tom
he says *who gives*
beauty fully

i fall asleep in
that elegance of
phrase thinking how
i am always at
a loss when asked
for an inscription

i will steal this
to use as my
own
      certainly
also i must think

to give photographs
instead of books

in the morning i
look again
         it says
to tom who drives
beautifully
          i am
relieved
       but will
send the photo
anyway
       inscribed

NINE TO FIVE

still they ask for poems
as blessing on their union
and we give them

unconvinced of efficacy
in fact discouraged
but they are not

they ask for poems
we give them

hoping hoping this time
it will flourish
despite the poem

the wonder is
we keep writing
they keep getting married
life goes on

GRANT US

the story of a forty-
three going on forty-
four year old man and
a just turned thirty-
one year old woman and
what they did not
know about themselves
or the world and what
they thought they might
find out if they could
make it through one way
or another is the title
of the novel in progress

it will take a great
deal of money if not
time and also effort

THE ROCK AND THE HARD PLACE

not the gull
picking the bone.
not the trees.
not the fog
rolling in.

no part of me
yet. i am
watching and
listening. i
am loosening.

no right to
respond. no
right to respond.
i don't know
these things
by heart.

the lessons
come hard, friend
keeping your
mouth shut unless
you know. not
to take in the
new places too
quickly, not
to write what
you don't know.

WAKING IN BED BY A RINGING TELEPHONE

Whose call this is I think I know.
Her voice is in Toronto, though;
She does not see me lying here
Naked, with a need to go.

Her little ears must think it queer
To hear me cough and wheeze so clear
As lungs wake up and rattles shake
The nicest waking of the year.

She gives my ears, for my self's sake,
The sense that this is no mistake.
The outer sounds I have to leap
Are starting trucks and screeching brake.

Her words are lovely, dark and deep,
So we have promises to keep,
And miles to go before we sleep,
And miles to go before we sleep.

DOING IT

isn't it beautiful
the act of printing

action of ink on type on paper

the fiber gives gently when
just kissed so the ink flows in

the poem acts spread out on paper

the letter says 'the god awful winds
knocked over & pulled up over
a hundred huge & lovely oaks so

i have been cleaning all this up
made a brush pile of dead branches
easy to break off came back
& proofed the poem acts'

reading the letter and
seeing the proof enclosed
knowing the catbox is waiting
to be cleaned i do it
                    i do this
shit isn't it beautiful
we go on doing both
we clean up
                we do this

LIFE STUDIES

the outer surface of
the thigh
when flexed
shows a groove
longitudinally
which corresponds to
the ilio-tibial band

the stroking of
the inner interior
aspect of the upper
thigh of a woman
leads to geigl's reflex
in poupart's ligament

in men this is known
as the cremasteric reflex

i learned all this
as we stood in the bookstore

watching women ride bicycles
up the slight incline
of the street outside
from my friend the owner
who translates medical texts
and thus has much to teach

i saw that the women's
breasts turned into dugs
as they leaned over
the handlebars so
i was reminded of
mother wolf her
dugs hanging down to
feed the hungry twins
romulus and remus
before they built us rome

our other friend is much
more primitive and hopelessly
obsessed with muscles
of the ass which ball themselves
to fight the uphill grade

he contents himself
with such lascivious thoughts

this was a pleasant
afternoon entertainment

the next day i slept through
that bright sun and was
awakened harshly by linguistics

a neighbor screamed:
please come in!
come back in goddamnit!
please come back *in*!

don't be a fucking cunt asshole!
for god's sake come back into the house!
i don't care how many rags you got on!
please come in!
i want to talk to you . . .

she had been sitting
in the car warming it up

the motor slowed and stopped
the cardoor opened and slammed
the housedoor opened and slammed
they were both inside

i was awake
                   and startled

no longer watching
safe with friends
learning
               i had been
enlisted in
a private war

and for that whole month
their car stayed parked
and i never once saw them

and the girls on bicycles
kept going up the hill
and we kept watching
from the bookstore

A LATE WINTER POEM

dying a slow death
dying small deaths
dying by pieces

what shall we tell

piece by piece

we who adjust
we who move on
we who move out
of the sun when
it burns us   we
who move into
the sun when we're
cold   we who know
enough to come in
out of the rain

we who adjust and
keep on living
and feel vaguely
less because of it

oh we who have
it all knocked up
because we give
inch by grudging
inch and keep on
living.   we who live.

FOR DANIELLE

although gesell would say
doesn't he always
she's far too young
isn't she always
i kept thinking
how williams saw and wrote

> A CHINESE TOY
> Six whittled chickens
> on a wooden bat
>
> that peck within a
> circle pulled
>
> by strings fast to
> a hanging weight
>
> when shuttled by the
> playful hand

and i thought
what the hell
are they ever the right age
if that's what we're
supposed to worry about
so i bought it

MEDITATIONS
for miguel grinberg / 3 may 1975

why should i be embarrassed
sharing my dishwashing
my grocery sorting
when you have come
from sharing his meditations

it is not so different
it is precisely how
his verses and mine
have lain cheek by cheek

the lesson of
the juggler of our lady
is constantly before me

i pick up the mail
after dropping the garbage
and you read my poems

share with me
i am a domestic poet
tomorrow i will pick up the toys
do the laundry
write a poem of the tits of the mother
who dances before me

WEDDING HAIKU

wind blows
                shakes island
holed up they warm each other
and winter passes

VINE DELORIA MEETS A PALESKIN

it's not the chasm
it's the bridge
i'm afraid of

that's why
i believe in trolls

FOR THOSE, THERE

that wide space
which is maine

that narrow space
the brain

that space
beyond space
the poem

they are
brought together

we are brought together

even far away
the poems ring

i hear them
they call me
to that wide space

FOR TOM BLACKBURN

metaphor is all
and all
when come to
metaphor

"to bear over"

the one act
which makes us
conscious also
brave deceitful
and the like

subjective self

writers have three
thousand years of
history so must
start by baring self
then move to
things bearing on our
selves and make those
things and self
more in the world

we never knew we
did it and can not
even comprehend that
doing yet keep on

it is a lesson to
bear over and over

words for things
for words for things
and still have them things
and still have selves
and have the world

FOR LOUIS ZUKOFSKY 1904–1978

when you tell the truth
they scream at you

when you lie
they scream also

when you write poems
they ignore you

when you don't write poems
it's like being dead

      when you die
      nobody tells us
                    again
      we are left to survive

      but we have what you have written
      and the words sing to us
      while we grieve that you are gone
      and that we paid too little attention

FOR THE O-YANKS 27 August 1979

this green square
tilted on end
is perfect geometry
in which the figures
move us with them
in their motion

there is no time
in this space
          it is

a dance which need
not end
            we dance with it
a cappella solo
eyes never at rest
taking it all in
the stretch of arms
sharp kick of leg
quick uncoiling
in response
            quicker
yet response to that

in this defined
and timeless space

THE WAY WE WERE
for jonathan williams / his fiftieth / 1979

that he used a lot of tabasco sauce
on one plate of scrambled eggs

that he looked like llud of the light
standing in at the plate

that he had the first hi-fi i'd ever seen
and fiddled with its controls
as if he were conducting it

that he played the first mahler i'd ever heard
the first bartok the first varese the first everything

that his books were so neatly arranged
but not by title or author or even subject
but by principles of design he learned in chicago

that when we were young we moved in the same world
and we lusted and loved together but not for each other we said
and we told each other the objects of our desire

that he was the first one ever to put his belief
in my words into words on a page to be sold

that he appeared and disappeared and appeared again
and has always come and gone in my life
while i have sat still in one place

that he has come into that place and pulled me out
and taken me to meet poets i dreamed of

that williams and zukofsky and blackburn were mine
because he brought me to them

that what we have talked about for almost thirty years
is music art baseball poetry and life

that we have drunk bourbon, wine, beer, homebrew, shine, and
                                        club soda together
in rooms, honky-tonks, parks, and executive suites

that he has lived his life and i have lived mine
and it took a gap of ten years to accept each other's

that he has been a friend for three-fifths of my life
and he has held a manuscript three-fifths of that

that he has one year and eighteen days on me
and that is enough to qualify him as older and wiser

that he brought culture to me
and made me eat it

that we are friends
and we will sit down together at the table

that is prepared for us wherever and whenever that is to be
and that at that table we will be greeted by the company of those
                                                        who can talk
vidal, li po, bobo, dizzy, and all

and we will eat and drink and laugh and talk our asses off
and play baseball and poems together
and have, in that place, all those objects of our desire
and once again we will tell each other about those
giggling like schoolboys up late at night
and finding the big world around us

FOR WILLIE SUTTON 2 NOVEMBER 1980

willie you went
where the money was
and began at
the age of nine

the report says
you robbed society
of two million
but i didn't know
we were the banks

of course it's easy
to speak of
glorifying thieves
but you did give
forty-three years
of public service
even did the laundry
at attica state
while nixon was
running for office

and you put on
costumes to
do your work
while the others
just put us on

and besides
like you said
the insurance
will cover this
and the rest
of our lives
has no such
insurance but only
bad actors
not knowing
the time they owe

A VILLAGE POEM

in the summer of '73
i'd had twenty years
in this place
                    my own
history

        a history
of places, things,
a piling up said one
a night-mare we
are trying to escape
said another

i sat in the white horse
with my son, nineteen,
beside me

             the last time
we sat together in a bar
he was five, and the bar
was the cedar tavern
and a man gave him
and his brother each
a dollar for a toy

what history had done
to the white horse was
to turn it too small
misshapen dingy dark
ceiling too close
not even memories

me only forty-three

i started to be cynical
i started to be sorry
i had brought him
i started to apologize

but i caught a look
in his eyes and i saw
he saw the ghosts
saw he saw dylan in
one corner, behan
in another, saw he saw
all writers everywhere
saw those drinking
their lives away
still writing their
words saw the white horse
was bright and real
for him
                  i shut up

and i remembered
my own history then

remembered the walks
twenty years ago
edna st vincent millay's
house or maxwell bodenheim
seen on the street
cummings in the back
of the eighth street
jackson pollock tackling
the eiffel tower in front
of the albert hotel
and all the bright moments

it's today for someone
else right now walking
in here young and eyes open
seeing the brightness

it's never, not
this particular way
for someone not here

it doesn't matter if
the crooked streets
the little houses and stores
or history or art
keep bringing them here

listen, some want to work
and will do so, even

     franz kline sat in the cedar tavern new hat on head bought at cavanaugh's
     he always dressed beautiful
                    pollock walked in talked drank got angry
     grabbed that hat threw it on floor jumped on it threw it

     ledge on top of the bar too far to reach
                          franz bought a round
                            a week later

pollock appeared again bought round sat talked stood up pirouetted said
look at my new raincoat just got at brooks brothers
                                                    franz said it is
beautiful
                    jackson bought more drinks sat drank got mad jumped up ran
outside ripped off coat stomped it in gutter threw into road under a cab
and came in
                    franz bought another round

it is history whether we
want it or not
it is what we learn from
it is where the paintings
come from and the poems

what? melville different, or
dreiser, poe, well yes maybe
james different but not
even that different

all young people come to find
a place and themselves
and their history and
to make their history
and to make their connection
the whole long line
of crazy people working
at work finding right places
where work is possible
where friends are possible
the whole long line yes
shakespeare had a place
villon peire vidal ovid
even homer singing
in some bar then

not that to drink
is to create or that

to be crazy either
not that to have friends
who do is to create
not even that to have
a place is to create
and certainly not that
this place is the only place
but that this place exists
and it might as well be
and we keep coming here
and using it for that
it is our place where we are
and it is the place where
the work gets done
as even tonight it gets done
and tomorrow when we are alone

because we have this place
and we believe in it

and it is still bright
and perfectly formed
and it is where we are

NEW SPACES

"seeing them i still open
still enclose myself in them"

TIME OUT

with even one day's worth
poems
            surrounded with these things
to find out what to care about

time time 'uncommitted free'

meanwhile sitting among all these things
all the time but only now to
notice and find out which

with only sons i see young
girls sprouting breasts while other
fathers see beards everywhere
darkening the chins of boys

meanwhile the papers are there to read
even when one doesn't have time

this is how one learns of the rebirth
of the everglades after fire and
how okefenokee is dying for lack
lack of that same fire
                        the swamp
does not dry out
                the dam built
to save timber outside the swamp
keeps the water too high
the swamp will not burn the natural
process of death and rebirth—are
you listening?—can not take place
the swamp is dying

        across the world
the egyptians curse the rooshians
for building the aswan dam they
wanted
        everyone forgot about
the silting
        the silt builds up
in the dam itself it no longer
flows with the spring flood to
make the land rich by the river

they forgot the silting in plans
for the dam damned engineers what
do they know or care of history
which is neither progress nor new

instead the growing land disappears
sucked into the current not
relaid year after year after year

now the banks crumble in
pull of the water as magnet

something else is new too
now the nile doesn't flow into
the mediterranean
        sea in the land
it seeps instead so the salt
creeps up that mouth that delta
that wellspring fouled

and the whole purpose of the dam
was to make power to make fertilizer
—camel shit!—to make the inland
deserts bloom
        and it does not make enough
to offset the loss from the banks
where there is no silt to come to rest

ebb and flood of the nile how many eons
we have disrupted destroyed

saying we even though they because
the only time we've ever refused
all for the wrong reasons of course
money and politics and ideology
and so the rooshians take the rap

we have forgotten how to be fathers
ought yes ought to watch breasts and
beards bloom we made them no? and
are entitled but further it is
our duty to notice it will keep
us from breaking the natural laws

we might hear occasionally these voices
and might have occasionally an idea
but the notion that we ought to be consulted
seems not to have occurred to anyone
not even ourselves although it ought to have

the notion that we might have ideas
and ought in any event to be consulted

every time myself this flooding
pouring out as if it were something

i'd forgotten it all in the damming
of the days and nights and never looking

more to have this—time time—and
the looking and to sit and he sd be uncommitted
so that the silt deposits and things grow

THE OLDER MAN THINKING OF KORE

the song rises

the skin shiny
and smooth

the belly free
at last

i am ready—

hi-yo!

she approaches!

FOOTPRINTS OF MAN-LIKE CREATURES FOUND

stopping to look
off to the left
hearing something
there
       "it gives a very
human aspect"

fifty-seven footprints
twenty are eight and a half
inches long
         twenty-seven
are seven point three

they figure to
four feet tall
and four feet eight inches

two people
walking along
singing a song
three and a half
million years ago

"by itself the ash
would not have retained
clear prints but it
appears it had been
wetted by a rain shower
and was slowly hardening
like plaster when
they walked over it"

walking along
singing a song
side by side

LESSONS I

the war was over
                   they found helen in
deiphobus' house

                he had taken her
there after paris was killed
                        against her
will

      she had given herself to paris
willingly enough

                deiphobus was
not what she had bargained for

so they burst
into the house
                  both menelaus and
odysseus
            to kill these two

                  but as
graves tell us
            "some say helen herself plunged
a dagger into deiphobus' back"

this and the sight of her naked breasts so
weakened menelaus in his resolve
that "she must die!" he threw away his sword
and led her in safety back to the ships

LESSONS II

the point isn't
that he fought that war
or vowed that she must die

it isn't even that
they left together
spent the exile in egypt
went home to sparta
together

            it is that
moment
            and the dreams
that led him to it

the dreams
when someone
leaves us for
another

and when
she is beautiful
in our eyes and
the other's and
the world's eyes too

so he raised his kinsmen
and their armies
and he fought
to kill her
and avenge his honor

the sight of
her naked breasts
ended this war

all through that war
he must have had
this certain dream
every little once in a while

this dream in which
he finds himself
again and again

he is bringing gifts
—beware a greek
bringing gifts—
yet bringing gifts
to her
            to ask
forgiveness
                since
we do decide we are
the one who's wrong

we ask forgiveness
in those dreams

while wide awake
we know how
wronged we are

in those dreams
we beg acceptance
and a smile

oh yes we know
that we have wronged

why else be alone

so alone we hope
to be forgiven
having done that wrong

in this certain dream
helen sits waiting

we open the gift
for her
              it
astounds her
and she smiles
then laughs

we too smile and laugh
as she accepts it
thus accepting us

so good in the dream
we wake sick with anger
having dreamed it

real anger that
somewhere deep
we still suck around
still beg

even
menelaus begs
for helen's
naked breasts her
smile and all

even when we know
the loss and time
gone
          know that
it's over
              dead

we want it that way
and we would not
change it
             still
we want love just
as it used to be

we want buttermilk
breasts that perfect
face that acceptance

the tender love
she had once felt
for us we thought

even knowing all this time
she deserves her paris
and he her
                perfect for
each other
                just as we
had thought we were perfect
once

even for the world
they are the perfect
couple coupled

yet we ask why
yet we dream why
yet we cry why
paris why him why
her
        where did i
go wrong

AFTER A POEM

i don't know if death
is an admiral in full dress

or a whore with skirt slit
up the sides of the thighs

or one of the queens

i don't know any more than
what does mother life look like

only that death and life
both exist and are

one is one or the other

the dancer is another story
and the fixed stare frozen
is another story also

they are the uniforms
i would like to know about
to recognize so I can
fall before or flee

ACTS

my son and i
walk out
in this cold october morning
toward his school

we hold hands

his other hand
holds a pennywhistle

he will use it
to accompany the guitar
in the morning singing circle

at each corner we cross
i am looking for you
while he and i walk and talk

i keep thinking
we will meet
at one of those corners
our paths intersecting
just as the clear note
of the pennywhistle
occasionally crosses
a particular chord
of the guitar
in the structure of some song

i keep thinking
in other words
that there must be a point
that we cross in common

and so this morning
we do meet

and walk together
half a block

he and i still
holding hands
you next to me
on the other side

one small moment
for you and me
to register our selves

and then later
after he is in school
and you are gone
i drink my morning coffee
and read the paper
again intersecting
this time with the world

i read that hugo zacchini
the first human cannonball
is dead

i read that all his life
he wanted to be a painter
and that after his retirement
he taught art to young kids

'yes, say for me'
he is quoted
'that my cannon
does me much honor
but do not
forget to add
that it is as a painter
that it is my ambition
to be known—

day by day
my cannon cannot give me
the thrills
that i can get
with my brush.'

lucky man who
day by day
first in malta
then throughout europe
then in the old garden

before me
a little boy
holding my father's hand

went one hundred and fifty feet
reaching an arc of seventy-five

where was my father headed
what intersection
was i going toward then

a flash
a puff of smoke
a roar
and he would go
hurtling through the air
in an idea
he conceived
serving with the artillery
in world war one

so i hurtle toward you
and toward this poem
aiming for some corner
of our lives
where we can meet
this morning

i do not know
whether or not
there is a net
it never occurs to me
to wonder about it

the flash smoke and roar
take the forms of
an alarm clock
and the radio
and a small child
needing his bottom wiped

oh this act also
will be carried on
by my son
just as his son
learned to enter
the mouth of the cannon

oh i also wanted
to do something else

oh i also learned my methods
in some previous wars

THE PROGRESSION

           all i know
           the body
           the poem

that strange land
the body
        maps abound
but i am lost there

      have known yours
      and yours
           and yours

        i forget them all
        not touching them

        having not once remembered
        hair
           not hair i lived with
        ten years
           then eleven

        not hair i see repeated
        on my sons
           not hair i find
        on collar or in bed

if you remember her hair
she is already an object to you

neither object nor person
or i would remember
              something

not even my own body
remembered
        save in touch

I

toe knee chest nut
is how i wash this body

       two days a week i saw a man
       to tell my dreams to

               that
       was so many years ago

       what i remember is i was
       always forcing myself into
       the cellar of my being
       because instead i wanted
       to ride always upward

     toe knee chest nut
     the game and song go

       i had to learn to go down
       in those dreams, into cellars
       of my being
             instead of upward
       into head and brain and
       intellect which ordered action

still cannot bathe
from top down
as others do
they tell me

skin crawls at thought
of washing groin after
face
     foot after
groin after face

i don't know why

II

phalanges = line of soldiers
tarsus = broad flat surface
metatarsus = at the back + tarsus
cuneiform = wedge-shaped
navicular = boat-shaped
cuboid = cube-shaped
talus = one of a set of dice
calcaneus = heelbone

all wrapped in muscle
pulled and held by
tendons
          sinews that
we walk by

covered with meat
with flesh
          with body
that we talk of

the foot supports us
as we walk away our lives
'men who spend their lives
walking and talking' is
the way he put it

wash every bone
with care
          the
cloth poised

the water runs

III

suspending part of her weight
from the bar above
the japanese lady
much smaller than us anyhow
and smaller still since lady
walks her toes up and down
the back
            it is the final stage
of the massage and they are
fingers on the back

            are like fingers indeed
            with much the same construction
            some names are different since
            they have evolved to different uses

a lady sat
right next to the flea circus
in the freak museum
beneath the penny arcade

her arms were folded
visible under her satin blouse

anything for a hype

it's a living isn't it

with her feet for hands
toes for her fingers
she wrote her name
lefty and then righty too

sold postcards for a nickel
signed both ways

            again and again i went back
            to watch her
                        wondered

what kind of discipline
could teach your toes to write
when you still had your fingers

what could drive you to it

they are like fingers
and the bones almost the same

IV

itchy feet
are not the same
as itchy palms

i don't like to walk

travel doesn't interest me

but i've been cursed
with itchy feet

if the body
contracts what it
deserves or wants
what are my feet
telling me itching
while i sit

contracted athlete's foot
at six while neither
athlete nor in
want of travel

have ridden with it
forty years or more

have often ripped
my toes apart
with painful scratching

have often winced
and shuddered in
the five and ten
when young when
faced with awful
posters of some
torn-up skin between
some model's toes

they always hung
just behind
the soda fountain

yet at night again
rubbed and rubbed
on bedposts and on
frame
          with fingers
and with nails and
with the other foot

relief from painful itching
was often promised

there is no relief
from painful itching
save the scratch

V

          this little piggy went to market
          this little piggy stayed home
          this little piggy had roast beef
          this little piggy had none
          and this little piggy cried wee wee wee all the way home

it is how we learned to count
so that roast beef has always
been a special food for me

and so that i always thought
it had to do with that
last pee to take for bed

and so that i always wondered
about the rhyme
                    how home
and none could match

the subtle pressures
of the culture

as the toes themselves
press against the
ground to hold us up

VI

one night
desperate
            cold and
stormy inside
she berated me
i did not know
how to make love

i felt her breasts
i rubbed her clitoris
i fondled soft her ass
perhaps then i
nibbled on her ear

oh the scornful look
oh the refusal

oh it's not enough
it's not enough

what of the ribcage
        though i knew one friend loved that
what of the arching back
        though i knew one friend loved that
the calves
    another
the knees
    another

all parts of the body someone said
'not erogenous'
                who said that

it was two in the morning
and the fight went on
until finally one by one
i kissed her toes
sucked them each
into my mouth
licked under in
the soft and hidden
parts
        rubbed against
the arch

she came then startled
and against her will
sitting in her chair

after this one night
she resisted my advances

she had learned that
her toes were erogenous

or my tongue was

and she'd thought
she had me beaten

VII

my own toes grow old
and no one will caress them

all that itching and rubbing
and walking and talking
and badly fitting shoes
have scarred them

now the nails grow strangely
curving round the ball
of toe
        impossible to cut

the nails are thick and hard

now i love them
because they are my own

we love only what
is our own
        or is
perfect in our eyes
in others

        there
is no middle ground

    i want someone beautiful
    and melting as has
    happened now and then

i will not settle

only those who move
in order to stop moving
settle

    others
cover up the ashes
and move on

VIII

    my first lover used her feet
    as well as head and opened
    up my pants by toes alone

    that also was erotic
    to a young man's sense

'ah, we were all beautiful
once,' is what she said
as she cut the roses

    i had grown enough not
    to be astonished that
    she could use her toes
    so well though she
    still had her fingers

IX

this little pig
went to market
five sons times
ten toes is what
it comes to
        not
counting my own

the feet we walk by

as we walk by
as we keep
touching ground

as we keep moving

FOR HAN YU AFTER ALMOST 1200 YEARS

"people say
when your teeth go
it's certain
the end's near"
he wrote

he wrote
"but seems to me
life has its limits
you die when you die
either with
or without teeth"

he wrote
"this is a poem
i chanted and wrote
to startle my children"

all the while
i was reading him
an unfinished draft
lay on my desk

"the breasts
of the young woman
from st louis
dance before him
and their nipples

rise to his hand
and also
her legs
stretch out
trembling"

i wrote
"he is
twenty years older
than the young woman
from st louis

"he was
raised in yonkers
and now
he is
almost toothless"

oh han yu
we don't change

not people like us

we're impossible
the women
keep telling us

we're incorrigible

we'll do anything

THE DREAM
for r.b.

diana goddess
moon sister mistress
once

      still haunting
dreams though it
is fifteen years

you have changed
and now hermaphrodite
you are testing me
as if the testing
then were not enough

i thought i had either
passed or failed that
time gone by
              as if
you were saying i
had not been tried
at all that time

see your phallos lifts
a two-bodied snake
joined at the center
of your body
a double phallos
to be taken somehow
all together by me
or as two apart

your breasts are
still full as i
remembered them
with the nipples

even larger
                    yes
we do remember

your sex is hidden
from me and i
remember that that
way
          though it was
always open to me
it was hidden all
the time as is the
way with all your
sisters always

now it is truly
hidden
                    in the dream
i could not get
to it
          though i tried

in the dream i
am working even
harder than before
to satisfy
                    you were
never satisfied
although i always
thought you were

you did not tell me
that you weren't
until the very end

what you said then
was that i brought you
closer than any person
had

you said that only
dreams had satisfied
you ever

so now
in this dream
my attention keeps
shifting so as
to satisfy you

breasts cunt double
phallos all before
me and i shift tensely
one to another seeking

it was hard enough
before when i thought
everything satisfied
and found that nothing
did and because i
learned that lesson
i start sure that
nothing now will

i have left the
dream goddess i
am talking about
a real past
a
history of
golden writhings
on your body
by my own

a body
i had seen as
heavy lead before
now something
new

transmuted
base to fine
learning its
capacities as
never seen before

but in this dream
i am suddenly aware
my ass is being
licked through all
of this, all
my difficulties
finding you
        it is
a man
    it is a
man i know

it is not a young
man or some similar
scenario
     it is
a man almost my
own age who licks me

like a satyr he is
tonguing out my
ass
    i tremble to it
as i tremble also
while i lick your
calm breasts and
nipples and the
double phallos and
your hidden sex

the satyr is intent
upon my rear

                    nothing
stops him
             let him be
my real friend as
in life but i
will not have it

in my dream i
object even as i
tremble to it

i cannot accept
his tongue or love

but i am intent
myself upon your
double phallos
as well as
your womanly
parts
          but in the
dream you are a
woman and he is man

i build a case within
the dream saying in
my head this means
i too am now complete
or almost anyhow
                          i
too begin to become
all
      i too begin
becoming one and whole

i make the argument
with myself within
the dream

    afraid
of loving my own sex
for what that means

afraid because i like
what he is doing

but perhaps the
argument is true
and it is not simple
fear
    then i am complete

if i can give and
take it all then
i will be freed
from your anima
i lusted for

i will be free to
love our mother as
i want to
     with all
my dreams and self

with all my poems and
words

    with this dream
then i will be
free
   my self

SCHIZOPHRENIA

i go out
to buy
a garbage can
hand beaters
a steam iron
a stew pot
a double boiler
scissors
and then
a new suit
and wellington boots

i am making
a new life

in between
i stop
to call you

you are angry
and i don't know why

the anger spews
from the earpiece

i call you again
after the boots
and the suit

it has eased a little
but you are still
very angry

i go on
about my new life

i have promised it
to myself
whether or not
you are part of it

in fact i think
you are scared
of this new life
and being part of it
and that is why
you are angry

it will be weeks
until you admit this
but now i do not know
and can only guess

there is another day
when you send
someone else to do
errands i know
you should do
and which i depended on
for an excuse
to see you and
to face that anger
if it could come out
face to face

by sending that
other person
you have made it clear
how little there is
you can say

oh well
i dust my
wellingtons
and make them shine
day by day

and i continue
to plan
how and when
i might run into you

A BEGINNING

we are here
in this place

we hunt these
new beasts

we take their
hides and their furs
to the island
to meet the ships

we were brought
to do this
              in this
new place where
fog covers all
too often

the sun tells us
how the year moves

when the sun rose
in the notch
the priest prepared
for its coming
it was the new year

now it is darker
it is four months later

we watch the sun
dying slowly now

it will die
faster and faster
and the dark will come

we will be alone
in this new place
without the ships
for the winter

building our piles
of furs and hides

we were brought here
for this
              the mother
came with us
her belly filled
by the father

              * * *

there are others here
with different faces

i have taken one
of their women
and they have taken me

we show each other
what we do

they know
these strange beasts
but i know the mother
and the father
and the coming

of the new year
and they
do not

her skin is a
different color
and the paint
on her face is
different too
and her hair springs
alive under my hand
and is black

i gave myself
to her
          my friend
gave himself back
to the mother

that has never
happened before

he asked the men
on the ships
to take him home
from this fog

they would not

i asked him
to take my woman's
sister
          he could not

he gave himself
back to the mother

he could not eat

the strange things
that grow here

and the bear
of this place
was different
to him
          he was afraid

i saw that this bear
was our bear's brother
and i welcomed him
as he welcomed me

and i eat
the strange things
that my woman
knows how to cook

          * * *

ah, even the rocks
are different here

still we can build
places to pray

and the mother of mothers
mother of heroes
the father of fathers
who is the sun
of the new year
all have travelled
here with us
in the ships
over the water

and the priests
have come
with the prayers

and we make
our homes here
and there will be
small ones too

to grow big
in this place

where we meet the
ships with our cargo

THE MAN OBSERVED
THROUGH THE KITCHEN WINDOW

Beginning the Portrait

it is monday morning.
he is washing
the breakfast dishes.
this is the easy day:
soft-boiled eggs, so
there's no frying pan
to be washed, and the
egg-cups and spoons
are easy once you remember
to run them through
hot water right after
eating. all that's left
are knives from the
jelly and cream cheese
and glasses from juice.
it is an easy day.
sometimes the children

drink out of paper cups
which should make it easier
but in fact they never
finish the juice which means
that the cups must be
carried to the sink, emptied,
then carried halfway back
to be thrown in the garbage.

       as usual, the realist painter
       watches all this through his own
       kitchen window. sometimes
       abstractedly. he considers
       making thumbnail sketches.
       someday there will be a painting.

this particular monday
is clear and warm. that
is better. perhaps today
he will get some work done.
there are, after all, letters
which must be answered.
mondays that are cold and gray
hold everything up all week.

even better, this monday
he has no erotic thoughts,
no fantasies or dreams
to consider and disturb him.
his motor is off, he is
only slightly angry, and
the world has not yet
fucked him up. so he
finishes the dishes,
rinses the sink, forgets
to wipe the table, and
curses when he remembers.
the world has started.
he wipes the table,

trying to catch all the crumbs.
half fall on the floor.
he ignores them and goes
to the children's room
where he takes the pot
from its seat, carries
it to the sink and empties
and rinses it and brings
it back. now he is ready
to work. his own bowels
stir slightly. he leaves
the kitchen again, the
frame of the window now empty
save for the dishes drying
and the usual impedimenta.

      the realist painter stops watching
      and turns his own head inward
      framing the scene in his head
      the window, the dishes, the impedimenta,
      the man discovered through the kitchen window.

The Concierge

occasionally he too looks
out the window while he
does the dishes. his eye
is caught, perhaps by a flash
of movement, or he hears
a noise. he turns his head
then and glances out and down.
he almost never looks straight
out across the courtyard
into a neighbor's kitchen
except by accident, since
he is not at all like his
friend the realist painter
who often spends long hours
watching, sometimes drawing,
sometimes just thinking.

he looks out only when something
attracts him, calls him to it.
sometimes it is a clutch
of women from the suburbs
come to visit culture
on a tour and he knows
their bus is parked, waiting,
in front of the building
though he cannot see it.
he sees a sculptor he knows
who's working as their guide
talking and gesturing. who
could know how to handle
these art-hungry women?
but the assignment pays
a little, and indeed the ladies
might just buy a painting
from one of the studios
they visit—or even
a contorted piece from
the guide himself! so
he does it for the money
one might say. why does
the poet do the dishes?

once, when he was still
married, he was in the
elevator, hauling his
laundry in a shopping cart
pushing the baby in
the stroller. a woman
from the building sneered
at him and made remarks
about his efforts. as the
elevator stopped to let
him off, he smiled and told her
he only did it to get his
wife to sleep with him.
the door closed slowly

but firmly the way that
elevator doors will do
and he kept the smile
all the way to his house.

nevertheless why is he
doing dishes? for the
money? does he know
he is posing for the
realist painter up there
in his window? he doesn't
even if quite often he
does feel he is posing
for something, someone,
when he stands patiently
alone at the sink.

sometimes it is the
children outside who lure
him till he turns to look.
not only his, but all
the children from the
building, fights beginning,
or loud and passionate
crying. his reaction is
immediate but not too
helpful, since all he does
is look. it is hard to
act sixteen feet above the
action, separated from it
by the window's glass.
and always he is brought
back anyway by the threat
of water overflowing.
besides, the window is
dirty, has not been washed
in six or seven years,
so that it is just not

satisfying looking through
it. he is not about to
swing himself out and
wash it, and the cost for
a professional is too
prohibitive. so the
window stays dirty, and
some sort of life
goes on outside it.
he does not think he
could spend his life
at a dirty window. he
is getting his chance
to find out at last.

Rinsing His Teeth

after his lunch, eaten
at the sink, sitting on
the kitchen stepstool,
after salami on rye with
mustard, and chocolate
pudding left from last night's
dinner, after all the lunches
eaten on jobs he used to hold,
business lunches, lunches
eaten at the desk, ah he
thinks, today i will eat
a pear. the pears are gone.
they are not in the
big boy's lunch, he
packed that himself,
putting in an apple.
the little one asked
for one last night, but
he refused him. someone
has taken the last pear.
he crumples. it is
almost a pose.

the realist painter in his perch
by the window perks right up.

but he is not allowed
this luxury of paranoia.
the crumbs of rye bread
and the lingering taste
of the chocolate pudding
bring him back, remind him,
and he turns to the sink,
turns on the water, and
takes out his teeth to
wash them. full dentures,
they remind him of his age,
of all the whiskey he drank
losing teeth, of jokes
about clean old men, and,
subconsciously, perhaps,
of the defanged vagina.
patiently he rinses both
his teeth and his mouth.

the realist painter finds this
a funny subject for a quick sketch.

he wonders if he could pull
such a painting off.

he wonders who might be induced
to buy such an obscene painting.

Making the Holiday Breakfast

he is not alone this
new year's morning. he
makes breakfast in good
company. the three year
old sits on the stepstool

chattering, and eats toasted
raisin bread while the
breakfast gets made, and
brings the silver and
the jam and creamcheese
and the toast to the table.
while the boy is busy, he
busies himself with bacon
and with scrambled eggs.
he adds grated swiss and
parmesan to the eggs as
he beats them. he is piecing
together a year. now the
eight year old enters, to
help to stir the eggs.

he is not alone in the new
year, he is piecing it together.

he has put last night's
coffee on to heat, there
will be two cups worth.
and he gets out the cream
and sugar and his cup.

      the realist painter is not yet
      awake, his window stands empty.
      no one looks out, looks in on
      this splendid holiday breakfast.

at the party he was at
the night before he saw
a bed built in a bathroom.
he thought as he looked
at it how nice it was
that there existed someone
more hung-up than he, but
now, this morning, he is
not at all that sure.

every one of them at that
party had sat waiting,
waiting for gaiety and
merriment to start, waiting
for the party's start. they
had thought that this was
the beginning of a new time.
at one minute before midnight
he'd had to remind them
it was the new year coming.

the kisses were sterile,
on the cheek and brow.
there was no passion at all.
nobody danced. he had
dutifully sat and sipped
his club soda, had not
missed the booze, had even
thought that next year
it might be cigars that
he was fighting. was that
a resolution? he had no
way to know or not.
he had smoked one joint,
had gotten a minor buzz.
mostly it had just kept
him awake. somehow he
was piecing together
a new year, a new time.

behind the empty window across the way
the realist painter slept on. in his dream
he watched people celebrating new year's.
they had clusters of white balloons he broke.

coming home from the party,
awake and alert on the
grass, he wondered at the
mildness of the night, and

remembered suddenly a
new years twelve years earlier.
the wind had whipped at
forty miles an hour, the
temperature had dropped to
ten below, they had four
blocks to walk and almost
couldn't make it. he could
not remember what it was
that year turned out.

they all sit down to eat.
they are all quiet as they do.

      the realist painter was still
      not yet at his window, watching.
      nevertheless, the year had begun.

bless the food we eat
at beginnings. we begin.

CITIES THIS CITY

the things they always complain of
coming from outside and again on leaving
there are so many of us crowded in here
and we are all so aloof and alone

we here are always alone
every city alone in this country
which has never learned to accept its cities
every city on its own alone and doomed
born to lose written on its walls

yet here we stay in it and keep coming to it
we keep pouring ourselves in and out

we light the skies with ourselves sometimes
sometime someone may be watching those lights

we are using ourselves people bodies
instead of trees and grass and earth
we eat people instead of eating the land
we watch love and hate bloom all around us
not weeds or flowers as in so many other places

we keep thinking we are making something
from our own bones and blood and flesh
and not like the others living off the land

we know that the oldest city was so
we know that the newest city will be so
it will always be the place the others use
while they keep complaining about it
while they send what they make from the earth
while they send what they can't use
while they send what they want to sell
for what we have to give them in return

they send their poets and their whores
their painters their conmen their dancers
their thieves their dreamers their murderers
and we add our own to these yes

maybe you cannot have one without the other
maybe indeed you need all in this city

i don't know if this is right
i only know the need to use one's self
to bet on one's self even when it's fixed
rather than watching things grow outside one
and then killing them and then piling them up

and when the ports and the crossroads
and the easy jumps across rivers

aren't needed any more for their commerce
the songs and the poems and the dancers
and the drawings of things imagined and real
which come out of the rub of people against people
will keep pouring out of the city's people
feeding the people who are angry feeding them

this feeding started in the first gathering
and will go on to the last gathering
because while the world builds itself in the void
people alone hunger for each other always

for whatever it is that only people can make
for whatever it is that only people can feed each other

THE HARDBOILED MYSTERY

dashiell hammett and maybe
raymond chandler too i am
reading you again after years
and yes i'd like to believe
the twists in the plots
came bubbling out almost in passing

i'd like to believe too
that you found those felicitous phrases
tripping off your tongue with no problems
but i know in all cases the lines
were sweated over to come perfect
or blurted out not knowing
what it was you were saying

then you were hung with it
had to follow it through
found yourself in positions
you didn't expect but had to defend
and you chandler popping those images
tell me straight weren't they simply evasions

didn't they just cover up the fact
that you didn't know where you were going
because i can see after the fact
that the plot line wasn't that carefully
laid down it didn't hang on index cards
neatly pasted on the wall before you
it got its own twists and twirls
until again there you were
waiting to find out what happened

oh my god how i'd like to believe
that living with a creative woman
dash was more for both of you
than hassling and moving in and out
and i'd like to believe also
that the drinking and the drying out
made sense as metaphors and
as a plot line too but i know
how hard it is living with any woman
or one's self and how you can
turn a corner and find the plot
gnarled up again and i know
how the phrases stumble and fall

i know where you come from
which makes me hope that heaven
is one long movie where it's all
straightened out so it will appeal
to everyone and everything gets settled
by the end and all the stars
know their lines and even the scenery is terrific

which is why this poem is for you
dashiell hammett and for you too
raymond chandler maybe and certainly
for me my own continental op
lost in this hardboiled mystery
in which nothing gets solved or comes clean

THE FOUR FATHERS

the first of whom
is clouded
               is
not to be seen but
felt in the dark night
is *phallos* simply
is insertion, jet
feel him

later, so much later
feel his skin
                 smell
cigars or sweat

whatever

he is not there

he fills her
or does not

out of him is built

he is dark and inside

then the second appears
nourishing
               he yells, shouts
he punishes and loves

he also takes the mother
but with deference
and is as frightened
sometimes as the child

the third father does
whatever the second did not
and does not do
whatever the second did

he tells secrets he has learned
and he creates his own mystery
since he is there for her
but also for himself

the fourth father is old
and we think him wise
and we find him a stranger
but we talk

oh i have been all
of the first three
and soon will be the fourth

each of the mothers
each of the children
know me differently

each has a different picture
folded in your heart

AROMAS

it stinks in
this bathroom
downstairs from
the organic restaurant
all fruits and vegetables
organic
        all meats
and poultry organic
and hormone free
and yet it stinks

and when the cats
shit in the clean box
that also stinks
while i make breakfast
for the boys and me

stinks stinks stinks
and as i turned down
to her she said
the plumbing broke i've
had no bath for three days
i stink
            she did

she was right
she stank
            the
acrid bite cut my nose
and i recoiled

she had not lied

so we coupled other ways
while that honest awful
stink hung on in mind

had she lied
                had
i not expected it
it would have hung
in nose as well

that night she bathed
and i went down

there was no smell but good
which itself was honest also

SUMMER SONGS

I

waiting for the afternoon
it comes
it is gone

II

fruit
flesh
in summer
all the same thing

i taste a cherry
i taste a plum
i taste you

juices flow

they taste fine
there's no difference

III

earth air fire and water
on the one hand
scissor rock and paper
on the other

earth puts out fire
fire burns up air
air dries water
water covers earth

whichever of us
was wrong
holds out our wrist

the other with
index and middle finger
together and extended
raps smartly

we are children
playing this game
but there are elements
of reality in it

IV

territory demands
we take each other's land
with knives
                    mumblety-peg
calls only for dexterity
and elegance of form

we play one or the other
as the need moves us

territory is ruined
if one gives one's land away

mumblety-peg fails
when one doesn't care

V

there are differences:
in winter i shower
because i want love
or because i've had it

in summer i shower
all the time
                    as if

plunging into the sea
had to do with
keeping my cool

VI

what i like
is seeing you naked

it is almost obligatory
in summer
                an impossible
favor in winter

suddenly i do not know
which to prefer
except that you are
more beautiful than
all the blackbirds
with their sheen-y feathers

VII

peaches plums cherries
grapes and berries

still lifes
on every table

i take
what i am able

CACTI

I

love comes
once a month
these days

i am not complaining

it drops on me
unexpectedly
just as rain does
on cactus
in nature
in the desert

it floods me
for a moment
forces new growth
drains away then
in sandy dirt

i am planted
in sandy dirt
insecurely

it is all
a conceit
of course

still
i am not complaining

i am stating
facts of my life
at this moment
and perhaps
from now on

i am
after all
still alive

i have survived
a long time

and i have watched
all the flowering plants
of my life
wither and die
because i did not
handle them
properly
or water them
as they needed
or perhaps
if the new thinking
is correct
did not know
how to talk to them

i am not complaining

i am learning now
that the cactuses
the succulents
even my crown of thorns
continue to grow
to survive
to flourish
without love
or water
more than once
every month

and it has taken
all this time

to learn this
and to learn
that they are my plants
as my life

yet it is true
the kangaroo vine
she left here
is still going

its tendrils reach
out to the lamp
down to the radiator
but this is an aberration
the exception
proving the rule

II

it is
opuntia rufida
the blind prickly pear
that first declared itself
as if in acknowledgment
of my own blindness

it refused to die
despite the fact
that i expected it to
and perhaps even
out of that expectation
encouraged it to

nevertheless
every time
i left this house
for any length of time
it sent out
new shoots

so that
when i returned
it had children
to greet me

they jutted out
and curved upward
at odd angles
and at odd junctures
from the main body

they were
bright green
even though
rufida itself
tends to blue
or gray green

now this cactus
will even grow
while i am home
and the shoots
continue to be
phallic in nature
just as i myself
have fathered
nothing but sons

cattle relish feeding
on the joints
of opuntia rufida
in the wild
and on its
small fleshy
bright red fruit
which i have never seen
but the plant
is supplied
with glochids

or thin barbed bristles
which fill the areoles
where spines would grow
in other cacti

these glochids
readily penetrate the eye
and blind the cattle
feeding there

next to rufida
there are two cacti
grafted together
as one

at the top
gymnocalycium
asterias
a bright orange globe
with tuberculate ribs

each tubercle swelling
just below the areole
so that the cactus
is called chinned

under it
cereus ocamponis
of which it is said
old stems turn
dull bluish-green
and the rib margins
become brown and horny

mine fits this description
it must be very old

the book also says
gymnocalycium

is self-sterile
in most species
and that hybrids abound
in this genus

next to that pot
on my table
a different variety
of cereus stands

it has just
been given to me
and i do not
understand it yet

it is tall
it is light green
it is shooting
a new growth
straight up
from its top

we watch each other
carefully
we will have to learn
to live with each other

behind this front rank
stand the others

to the left
echinocereus
a hedgehog cactus

it is self-contained
and silent too
as are all cacti
but has attracted

from somewhere
an unnamed succulent
which has sprung up
beside it

the succulent
is very young
but already tall
with small thick leaves

it is ready
for its own pot
but i am afraid
to transplant it

it is not
related to
the jade or
happiness tree
as they call it
in england
which grows
separate and distinct
in its own pot
a handspan away

this succulent
i am told
should have its
leaves wiped clean
every fortnight
but i do not believe
this happens
in nature

new york city
is not nature
and we do

the best we can
in its grime

since it and i
continue to flourish
i credit such happiness
as we have
to this jade
doing its best
in this house

i told you
i am not complaining

at the rear
of all these plants
rearing proudly
is euphorbia
my crown of thorns
which i rescued
from friends who
despaired of it
tired perhaps
of its stance
or its obduracy

having watched
the cacti grow well
i was emboldened
to try this one also
and brought it home
even though then
i did not know
its name

i was born
in east virginny
to caroline
where i did go

and there i spied
a fair young maiden
her name and age
i did not know
says the song

this plant
grows tall
with thin green leaves
small sharp thorns
and a woody curving stem
still it is
a succulent
i am told
and it has
a rare
hard
and terrifying beauty
that makes us equal
as we face each other

III

these plants
enlarge my landscape
and make it green

no this green
is not leafy
or flowering
it is not
the beauty
many depend on
but it does not
leave me
and it gives hope

spikes
spines
thorns

thin barbed bristles
protect it

and when you touch
we hold on

we do not
grab you

you must
come to us

like the rain
once a month
out of nowhere
out of blue
and beautiful
skies that rain
otherwise
on leafy
flowering plants

this is why
i am not complaining

i am learning
how to live

i am learning
i am neither rose
nor weed of the field
but did not know that
and suffered long
trying to be such
trying to grow that way

i am not complaining
i thrive

even though
i grow older

i grow stronger

the only ones
that i hurt
these days
are the ones
who do not understand
and try to
grab me
or come to eat
too ravenously
and are blinded for it
or those
who laugh
to see my
brown and horny
rib margins
my colors of
blue or gray green
and cannot accept
that this
is beauty also
and a way
to keep living
in a hostile
climate
in a soil
that would not
support an ordinary beauty

those who cannot accept
another way
to live

HOUSES

eighteen years ago
i left your house

it was your house

yes i brought home
the money
                we
did it that way
in those days

now again
i am showering
in your house
            "her bath, which she takes
            because he wills it so. . . .
            in his tub. in his water. wife."
            was even more years ago

                i do remember
                and i don't

getting undressed
i saw a silk robe
hanging behind the door

and the jars of oils
the soaps and powders
lining the shelves
beside the door

all in neat order
beautiful things

things beautiful
by themselves

and things beautiful
on your body

i thought how all
that i have loved
all that i have missed
is in this house

don't misunderstand me
i am not speaking
of romance
or rekindled love
or even second chances

nor is it a new obsession
with neatness
from one who's always
been the other way

if anything it might be
a lesson for younger lovers

perhaps even
for the ones
i come here
to see married

our first son
and his beloved
as if that action
by our child
allows you
to invite me
and me to accept
and that is why
i am in this house
far from my own

far from that house
i have learned
my own lessons
in building

in any event
a lesson
here also

      in first love there are things
      we grow to as a habit
      and will never be happy
      without again
               sexual appetites
      change
         it is easy
      to grow cramped and leave

      still i say again
      no matter what reason
      for the ending
             there are things
      we grow to as a habit
      without which
      we will not be happy

so it is
that years ago
i learned to love
your ways
so clean and neat

ways that cared
for beauty
and were beauty
and were
without
compulsion

            they happened
around me
without my knowing
and they were
caring ways

i've smiled at times
these eighteen years
realizing that
the only reason
i have folded up
my washcloth
in my bathroom
is because
you wanted it
that way
instead of crumpled
                          while
all that is remembered
of our sex
are bits and pieces
of some short-lived scenes

no touches
no movements
underneath me

a few sighs
or groans
a few importunings
one to the other

a picture of your breast
or thigh or face or hand

but i remember
very well
the house

you gave me
and see it
here again

perhaps this is why
i am so pleased
that i have changed
to see it
through the eighteen years
for what it is
and what it was
for me
        not that
you have not changed
it's clear you have
it's clear we both have
but this part of you
has not
        and the part of me
that sees it has

        * * *

now it is after the shower
and i have changed
in a much simpler sense

i am in some
new-found finery
a fop or dude
inside my western shirt
my shiny boots
and all the rest
as you have never seen me
and i feel i fit
in your house now
a stranger perhaps
because i am so proper
where as your lover
i stuck out

                    it is
the proper way to visit
i am saying

but on your shelf
among the oils
and powders
is the frog
i bought you
our first christmas
twenty-five or more
years ago

i see it now

made of brass
a candleholder
on his back

                    i knew
you wanted it
i saved the five
or seven dollars
that it cost
                    i'm glad
to see it now
                        it means
you really wanted it
it wasn't just a fancy

you kept it with you
and you use it now

there is a stub
of candle in it

perhaps some nights
you bathe yourself

by candlelight
                  i
see you that way

long baths as
i remember
                while
i lay in bed
reading
        or wrote
that first book

the one with poems
about you bathing

or just waited
in our bed for you

the waiting was not
always good
                it
destroyed the marriage
i have sometimes
thought
        but not
the waiting
while you bathed

that was part
of what you gave me
as i lay in bed
and dreamed
            a sense
of preparation and
of love and care

it was the other waiting
caused perhaps by what

i did to you or
what you thought i did

then after a while
i could wait no longer
and i went
                you
were just as happy
and that pain
is gone now

i remember only
there was a woman
of rare beauty
                a wife
who bathed herself
so slowly in my tub
that i wrote poems
about it
            in that first home
i ever had
            a home you gave
to me long years ago

        * * *

before the shower
i had taken a nap
in the guest room
of your house
                i
dreamed of us
of course

we were naked
but only from our waists
on down
        as   if to say
this is where we are

right now
                with the sex
outside and open

we were so afraid
in those days
and we didn't know it

in the dream
our tops were covered
our brains under cover
covered prettily
to face the world
and each other

perhaps that
might have worked
if we had known it then
to cover up our brains
and let our sex hang out

but we didn't know it
and we kept on talking

so i woke from that nap
this afternoon in your house
at peace with the dream
despite its sexual content
which aroused me
                it was
not you so much as
talking to myself
the good doctors
tell us that

at peace i went into
the bathroom for my shower
where i found my past

and was at peace
with that too
as i am now in my house
writing this to you

the house i've fought
my way through to get to

this house which is
not so clean and neat
as yours
                i am a man
i need a woman's touch
might be the pity of it
but i've learned to build
without it
                but now can see
how pleasant such things are
and where they come from
in me
        that is what
i did not know
                    and what
i now do know
and will remember

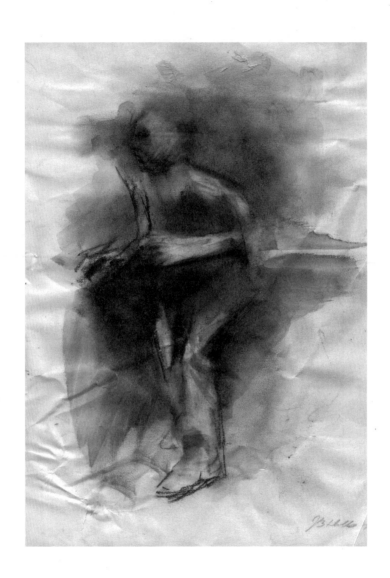

Notes Toward the Definition of David

BATSHEBE SEEN

Let not my beauties fire
Enflame unstaied desire
Nor pierce any bright eye
That wandreth lightly . . .

oh summer and a summer love
and i king
        eye
not wandering lightly

this old familiar story
middle-aged poet (king?)
puissant (pissant?) watching
(ogling?) younger woman
taking off her clothes

says in his defense:
we were to go swimming.
it was only the second time
we'd met. our eyes
had said something
the first time, too.
we met to go swimming.
she drove to my house.
it was warm, very.
but by the time she got there
the weather'd 'turned around'.
she was in a light jumper,
i thought she had her suit
on under it, something
about the way the fabric
pinched and poked where
the nipples would be, it
looked as if she had
her suit on underneath.
but now it was colder

and she wanted to change.
we'd walk instead of swim.
i gave her the other room
to change in, the door
was only a drape. the drape
hung only halfway really
unless you dragged it shut
and hooked the end tightly.
she didn't. i sat on my bed
on this side of the drape
to change my own clothes.

eyes deliberate but swift
saw breasts appearing
slender 'narrow restless
ungathered' that son
of a bitch had looked too
you betcha
        another
poet king peeking also
somewhere sometime always

she was stripping off
her jumper then for
my wandering eye
        the
only thing she wore
a bit across the hips
she had long legs

she had good legs
naked breasts my
heart leaped so then
don't tell me you don't know
this
    who leave the drape
unpulled
      stand naked on
the rooftop bathing
some will tell you later

but i was ashamed
i stole that look
all the while that
i was glad i stole
that look
                  like david
king and all and leerer

and all that afternoon
in that cold air hungry
to touch or kiss her
images of breasts and all
legs and hips and thighs

yet waited one more
afternoon to meet

yet spent that afternoon
ashamed i peeked and
warmed with sight of woman
young i wanted just
like david king who also

peeked through curtains
to watch her naked
as she showed herself

showed herself to him to me
showed herself again to us

KINGS

many women lie in my father's bed. some mornings
when i am awake before he is i let myself visit him and i see
for myself. he sleeps in a cold room. i do not always like that
and so i do not always visit. when i was younger, when he still
slept with my mother, i would go in that cold room on cold
mornings and climb in the bed between them. now i am
too old for that, even on the mornings when he is alone.

one morning when i went in i saw a small blond head next to
him on the pillow. i thought it was my younger brother, but
it wasn't. now, the other day, my younger brother went in
there, and he saw a small brown head on the pillow. he told
me later he thought it was me. he does not seem to mind these
women as much as i do. this particular day, after he saw it wasn't
me, he still climbed in bed, and he wrestled with them both. he
said she was a nice lady, and he named her 'momma rat'. this
was probably because my father calls him 'mouse' sometimes.

so far as i know my father has not slept with any women with
red hair—but the oldest of us, my first half-brother, has red-blond
hair, and once, while we were talking in his room, he told me his
hair was the same color as his mother's. his mother was the first
woman my father ever slept with. now she lives far far away. i am
told she came to see me once when i was five, and that i was asleep,
and that she looked at me in my bed, but i do not remember this.

one night i was trying to sleep in my room when i heard my father
very loud. i snuck out and looked down the hall and i saw him. he
was dancing, by himself, and a woman sat and smiled at him while
he did. he seemed strange, like he was drunk, but i know he doesn't
drink any more, because he stopped when i was three, because it
was making him die.

i remember then that i didn't see him for a week while he was with
the doctors, and when he came back he just sat and stared a lot for
a long time and he moved very slowly and he was very nervous.

but he got better after a while and then sometimes he played with me. sometimes he yelled at me, too, and he had never done that when he was drunk all the time. so it was better this way i think because he played with me and hugged me too, and when he was drunk he used to talk right through me and it was as if he wasn't there or i wasn't there i don't know which. i loved him but i didn't know which. i think my mother loved him too when he was drunk, because it wasn't 'til after he stopped drinking that she cried and yelled a lot and then she left.

anyhow, now he was dancing, a great ungainly person i could hardly recognize as my father. every once in a while he would stop and hug the woman and she would kiss his neck and ears and he would slip his hand over her breasts or her rear. finally i went to bed because i didn't like to watch even though i wanted to see what would happen and besides i started to fall asleep and i was scared he would catch me too. so i went back to my bed and fell asleep. and in the morning he was very grumpy when he woke up, which was very much later than he usually did. and he didn't talk much to the woman either. i can't remember what her name was, but her hair was dark brown and long and she was thin with small breasts and she only came back one or two more times.

my father is old. i suppose everybody thinks their father is old when they are a kid, but in fact my father *is*. he was old when i was born, and then he was older still when my little brother came. but the women in his bed that i have seen are both young and old. it doesn't seem to matter.

i am told that my mother was a young woman when he met her. he was at the same large party that she was at and they did not know each other. she was with a woman friend of hers and he was with a bunch of his men friends. he went to get himself a drink and he passed the woman who would be my mother while she and her friend sat there at the party. they were both very beautiful. he stopped to say hello to them because they were beautiful even though he did not know them and he told them that when he came back with his drink one of them would dance with him. so it was

my mother who danced when he returned while the other stayed
sitting. i know her, too, because she is still a friend of my mother.
she has a child four years younger than me, a beautiful little
blond girl. i do not believe the little girl is my father's
child, but i do not know that for sure.

sometimes when i visit my father's room on those mornings i
catch a glimpse of some of the body of one of those women, but
the only woman i have seen all naked is my mother. we used to
bathe together. i remember when my little brother was in her
belly, and i said her belly looked like a pumpkin. i made her
laugh when i said that, but later, lying in bed, later that night
and still awake, i heard her screaming at my father that she did
not want to look like a pumpkin. i wanted to tell her she was
beautiful but i was supposed to be asleep so i did not.

it is from looking at her that i know that she, and all women
she tells me, have a great thatch of hair where i and my father have
cocks. she says it hides her flower, but my father calls it a cunt.
i have heard him say that listening at night. in school we say vagina.
and i know that my cock goes in there, whatever it's called, to make
a baby, but i don't understand it yet. my little brother just had a
lesson in school about a lady giving birth to a baby and they
showed him what happens inside when the baby is first made. he
says that they told him the father's cock puts little wigglings like
tadpoles into the mother, and they swim very fast to the mother's
thing inside. he says the mother's thing they told him is just a
big egg that sits there. bam! a tadpole gets in, and the
baby starts to be made. i don't understand it.

i used to get very nervous about all these women he sleeps with—
i guess i still am. but one day he talked to me about them because i
had acted bad, he said. i didn't think it was so bad, but i guess i was
mean to one of them. he wasn't even sleeping with her, he was just
talking to her on the street. they had met walking and he kissed her,
on the cheek, and then they started talking. i was just standing
there and i wanted to get on home with him, and i didn't
know who she was, so while they were talking i just looked

right past her and said, "who's she?". the lady laughed when
i did that, but my father looked at me hard and said, "why don't
you ask her?" and so i did, but it was hard to do, to talk right to her.
i don't like talking to people i don't know, and especially if they are
women my father might be sleeping with. my father says if i don't
talk to people how will i ever know them? so i asked her who
she was. she told me her name and said she was just someone my
father knew and hadn't seen for a long time and that she was just
a friend of his. i guess that meant she wasn't sleeping with him.

so when my father talked to me about it later it all just came out.
he asked why did i always act that way and i didn't know it myself
but i said, "i don't want any more brothers." my father laughed
then and said, "i don't want any more sons either." he said that
most ladies he knew didn't want to have children either,
but i know what i'm talking about.

he keeps telling me not to worry. still, i do. it's hard not to.
there's my biggest half-brother, the one with the red-blond hair,
and there's the next one, who's my friend too, but doesn't live here
any more because he's out in the big world he says making his
fortune and sleeping with his own women friends. and
there's my middle half-brother who lives far away
with his mother. i have enough brothers and
i don't want any more.

i want to play ball and draw pictures is all that i know i want.
and my younger brother wants to be an artist also.

OLD DAVID

i found a father
he went mad

i found a brother
he was killed

i had wives and wives and wives
women and women

i had sons and daughters

the faces become one
repeating and repeating

she was a woman
i was a man

we slept together
we had a child

michal was given to me first
abigail was the first to come to me
abishag was given to me last
bathsheba also i remember

the rest are one face
and i am cold

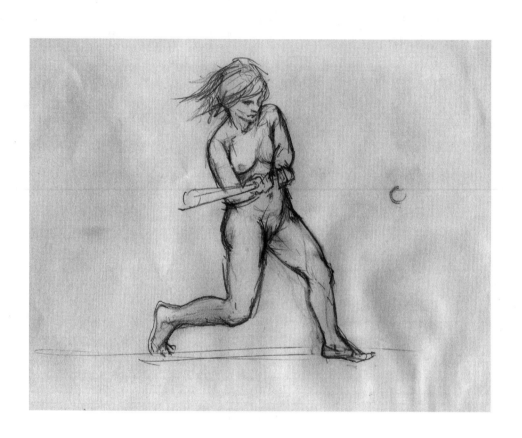

WHY NOT

for the friends who have
taken me in and
sheltered me and
fed me so well
in laurinburg
and bar harbor
and oneonta
and buffalo
and henniker
and rochester

"seeing them i still open
 still enclose myself in them"

PREFACE

there has been a welter of talk about the function of art, its
meaning, its value, and, indeed, its relevance. the talk has gone on
for ages. just the other night i heard an artist—a sculptor, but the
discipline makes no difference—say that the most important
"meaning" of his work is that which the viewer bring to the work.

i recoiled in horror. one hears this refrain over and over again: the
professor of poetry who says that only the sound lasts, while the
sense changes; the critics who, these days at least, seem intent on
proving a case for themselves at the expense of the work under
hand, and therefore insist that there is no meaning beyond the
language itself; the audience which has been educated to believe
that "it means whatever i want it to mean"; the artist him or
herself who responds by saying "it doesn't matter what i wanted it
to mean, as long as you respond somehow."

i meant for these poems to mean things. i had things to say in
them. i hope they say those things to you. i don't mind if they say
other things to you, or make it possible for you to say other
things; both those responses are legitimate as well as time-
hallowed. but i damn sure hope i've written these poems in such a
way that you can "believe" them; if i say it is snowing, or i am
looking at a desirable woman, or it is hard to face breakfast
without any teeth, you will understand them at that level at least
and move on from there.

every poem we remember has to do with real things, no matter
how far the poet's imagination or invention takes it from those
real things. we remember the poems because we have had
responses triggered in us by the poet's perception of those real
things, as well as by his imagination and invention. every poem is
an investigation of the world we live in, the way we live, and the
way we treat ourselves and others.

i hope also that the poems allow you to play as they have allowed
me to play——with language, with ideas, with juxtapositions,

with life. because human beings play, and that play makes living possible. perceptions of the universe are play, must be play. and there are no better examples than poems or any form of art.

that is the meaning of these poems, generally. the specific cases can be understood, always, on that level. the language exists to help communicate those investigations one to the other. whether the material communicated is important is not important, because time and people will winnow out the "unimportant." but the thins themselves, in fact, whether love or hate, war or peace, are always important. we are drawn to these investigations, and we learn from them. if we handle them badly, we produce bad poems and those are forgotten—or "unimportant"—or, perhaps, just meaningless.

i hope that these poems mean something to you. not each poem to each reader, but one or some to each. if they do act in that way i have succeeded as a poet—and as a human being. and the poems will be "important."

THE CORRESPONDENTS

I

dear sir i
wld like to see
this poem in
print perhaps we
can do business

II

dear sir enclosed
are a few thoughts
you could think
on these are
average i have
more some better
some worse perhaps
you could start a
series of thoughts

THE TEACHER

battered by sensibilities
i pretend the poem is easy

but it is not easy not for
me not for you ever at all

i give you simple rules
and if you follow them
the poem is simple

i give me complex rules and
again the poem is simple
because the complexities

are as bad themselves as
any of my sensibilities
and they writhe and intertwine
until all i am left with
is the blank landscape the
simple landscape the landscape
covered with cliché alone

you all pay attention to
my simple profundities
and do not understand the
simplest fact which is
that despite its simplicity
the poem is a difficult thing
and we are prey to all
its various vagaries and
vagrancies and shifts of
time and space and meaning

battered by sensibilities
in front of the class i
take deep breaths pretending
the poem is easy to write
and you write simple poems
and i praise you for them
and wish i could reach as
simple a conclusion as
i pretend is there before us

it is but still the sensibilities
batter me and batter the poem
and the poem winds on itself
and becomes complex no matter
how simply i conceive it

and becomes simple no matter
how profoundly i reach for it
in the midst of its complexities

if you want bread love a baker
says the old folk wisdom and
that is simplicity enough and
even perhaps sensible also

THE LADY

in the dream
she comes to me clothed
and we talk

now i remember
when we met
her nipples
at the fabric
of her blouse

later later
after the dream
she is smaller
plainer
          the dream
is still strong

THE FLITCH OF DUNMOW

a flitch or gammon of bacon
awarded when the claimant knelt
at the church door on two sharp stones
and swore that for twelve months
and a day he had never had
a household brawl nor wished himself
unmarried
                    a custom instituted
by the noble lady juga in 1111
restored in 1244 by de fitzwalter
re-restored in the 19th century's second half

eight claimants stand remembered

richard wright laborer of bawburgh near norwich 1445
steven samuel of little ayston essex 1467
thomas ley fuller of coggeshall essex 1510
william and jane parsley he a butcher much-easton essex 1701
thomas shakeshaft woolcomber weathersfield essex 1751
a couple name not recorded 1763
john and susan gilder tarling essex 1773

bless them all
shakeshaft and those unnamed

those sharp stones hurt
as truth hurts too

but oh a year of peace
and no regrets for it
and bacon in your belly
as reward for it

QUATRAIN

now they have cut a life from each of us
but mine was death to life and yours a life

we gave ourselves but could not take for us
so the fullness of our bodies took the knife

FOR A PAINTER BEYOND HAZARDVILLE

driving back from your house
we passed this sign which showed
the cutoff to hazardville

you are forty miles beyond it
deep in the valley of risk

you dare you have told me
to be beautiful
                    to feel things

you look at the hills now
as well as the people
and as well as the colors and shapes

that is a risk worth taking
when we have learned to see

in the valley of risk
feeling comes hard

beauty is in the eye of the beholder

in the valley of risk
beyond hazardville
                    past dare
one takes one's stand
and gives as good as he receives

in the valley of risk
streams run
          we choose
to see them or not

we wade and cross over
frolic or paint the purling water
figures appear after the decision

paint them
                bellies get larger
paint them
                if children come
send them out to the brook

the work must be done

in that cold water will they not
learn to feel and to see also
and to touch the shapes

      * * *

when we grow older
it becomes a verbal act
in which the shapes
must be formed exactly
and the words understood

we take our risks
we are beautiful

other people see this
and they walk up to us
in libraries
                they comment awkwardly
we smile with grace
            we
have learned that also

* * *

do not go below hazardville
stay
        stay in the valley of risk
the beauty surrounds you like high mountains
it is your duty to paint it
while i strive for the words to say it to you

our children play in the brooks
that cross this landscape
what do they know about it

all and nothing
            they will tell us
when we have grown too old
when we grow too old to dream
when poems and paintings stop

THE LESSON

i swear that
this morning
nathaniel said
setting his compass
over the paper
this will be
either a
very large moon
or a small planet

it is
a distinction
i cannot draw
no matter how
i sharpen
my pencils
no matter how

i stretch
and set
my head

-ETIC

aesthetic
ascetic
athletic

cosmetic emetic frenetic

genetic hermetic kinetic

magnetic mimetic

pathetic phonetic phrenetic
poetic prophetic splenetic
synthetic abietic

alphabetic anaesthetic

antithetic

apathetic arithmetic
dietetic energetic
exegetic

geodetic homiletic masoretic

parenthetic sympathetic

theoretic antipathetic biogenetic

peripatetic

abiogenetic

o
no
ma
to
poetic

THE THOUGHTS OF THE FAT MAN'S FATHER

the fat man's father
lusts also but the
fat man does not believe this
                        the fat
man's ladyfriend does

    * * *

the fat man's father
has a lean and hungry
look
        he is not trusted

    * * *

the fat man's father
has an idea of the universe
but it is clouded

his life obscures the idea

    * * *

it is hard to see
that he moves still he does
and his universe
changes accordingly

    * * *

the fat man's
father's daughter
is slim and beautiful

she writes him often
and the letters sing

his heart leaps in
his fatherly body
whenever he hears them

inside every father
is a beautiful daughter
trying to get out

        * * *

for the fat man's father
love is always just
around the corner with
a husband or slightly
crazed mind standing between

        * * *

the nature of
the fat man's father
is such that
he goes away
satisfied with
whatever he has

he takes what
he can get
and stuffs it
so to speak

it is neither
relaxing nor
relaxed
        it is
what he does

THE NEW LINE

talking to mary
telling her
an old line
as joke
but meant

we'll have to
leave it there

which is sad
but like they say
you can't make
an omelet
without fucking breaking
fucking eggs
those bastards
who keep on talking
keep on talking about

THE WORD

no matter what book
i use to level
the record player
or i put under
the end of the couch
where the leg is missing
it is always needed

like right this minute
i need the history
of the bugatti and
the lesser works
of gertrude stein

it's always the same

"if you were going
to repair your house
which books would you take?"

do not list
more than eight

BILLIE'S BLUES

i can't get
started easy livin'—
my last affair don't
explain gloomy sunday

how am i to know what
a little moonlight can
do as time goes by
in my solitude?

crazy he calls me
when a woman loves
a man fine and mellow

that ole devil love
he's funny that way

why was i born
foolin' myself all of
me body and soul
night and day

these foolish things
me, myself, and i

i wished on the
moon i'm yours
lover man on the
sunny side of the
street
       let's do it
my man until the
real thing comes
along
       i can't
give you any thing but
love—ain't nobody's
business if i do my
old flame
          lover
the man i love
come back to
me summertime

i cried for you
strange fruit
        you
go to my head

i got a right to
sing the blues
i cover the
waterfront

embraceable you them
there eyes mean
to me pennies from
heaven
      good mornin'
heartache if you
were mine

i'll be seeing
you
    you showed me
the way i'll get by

i love my man
       i
must have that
man more than you know

god bless the
child
    miss brown
to you

VARIATION ON A THEME BY WCW

lustful creature
full of sin and song
lustful critter
are you never satisfied
lustful crayther
never get enough
o that wonderful stuff
hello central give me
doctor jass he's
the man who's got it
mean he hass
      the more
i get it more
i want it seems
i page ole doctor jass
in my dreams
lustful creature
lustful creature full
of sin my song

TWO HAIKU TO BE READ EITHER ONE FIRST

ART

blue-green city bird
tumbling loosely in the street
you looked like a bag

NATURE

blue-green torn kraft bag
tumbling loosely in the street
you looked like a bird

THE CHARM

this is a charm for entering the tower
the tower stands carved in ivory
blue skies and white cumulus pile behind it

but that cloud is boiling behind it
soon lightning will flash from it

oh we are all born fools innocent and smiling
while our dogs frisk at our feet
we walk off the edges of cliffs

we fall safely to the plain at the foot of the tower
we look up it is there before us
phallic threatening alluring

that is the day we have to climb it
the dog left behind
the innocence the smile left behind
even the id surmounted

what happens is in the clouds
the cloud boils up covering the sky
the lightning will strike to the middle of the tower
the tower will crack and crumble and start to topple

people fall from the windows
again there are smiles on their faces
halfway up halfway down they are falling

you may think this is a terrible card
saying the tower falling presages tragedy

it is a way to move on to new things
it is a way to learn how to survive
it is learning how to live through even the crumbling tower
here are people who survive it

it is only the crumbling of something we've made
i repeat those falling again have smiles on their faces
a little different from the smiles they had before
but they are smiling again falling not to their doom

it is the card we must pass through

first you must enter this tower
the clouds boiling behind it
the storm building up even with a clear blue sky

THE GARDEN

i have taken
to buying flowers

i had inherited
three vases
                    memories
from my childhood

one slender brass
one chinese a
touch of class
one forties awful
decorated glass
with glassier flower
buds stuck on

i fill them weekly
with a few bucks worth
and i have begun
to see them
                    irises
made for watercolor
or watercolor for them
peonies so lush
they fill the room
opening and fading

daisies last

sweet william
has too many
variations
                    i
grow confused by them

statice stands
tulips bend
lilacs die too soon

these are city-bred
conclusions as i know

but they are conclusions
in a world made new

where flowers never were

SPRING

this letter
is long overdue

it is late in spring
and it was promised
in february

it is on the second
of that month
that persephone
begins her journey
up to earth

the letter is not
for her but for
her lover dis who
as lawrence tells us
sends that spring
chasing at her heels

she flees his dark house
and he sends flowers
snapping at her heels

friends glorying in
spring in the country
mistake me also

as we mistake dis
and send letters
to tell each glimmering
change of season
as if it did not happen here

so the letter is
to say we know it here
as well
              that spring
comes just as surely
every time it should

i announce spring
in the city

flowers on bethune street

and on bank
                in little
plots of earth exposed
around the trees that
stalk the sidewalks

snowdrops first as usual
then croci now tulips
daffodils and where space
is wider cherry trees

others have pictured
this place differently
they feel sorry for us
locked
                but dis knows
cities too
                the flowers
come snapping at her heels
even here

so i announce spring

SUMMER

the wind
has an edge
this evening
it turns around
and around
pivoting

now it comes
from the east
and is cold

the sun has gone down

two hours later
it comes from
the south
         i sweat
in my jacket

you also turn
around and around

you say it is over
yet we fall
in each other's arms

it is warm again
it is cold again

the wind turns
on its pivot
endlessly

LOVESONG

it would be different
those browned thighs
that patch that patch
the tiny white between
the whited thighs
the way the blouse falls
the way the blouse lies open
lies half-closed
the way the straps hide
and disclose where the straps are
the way the bending lifts the
blouse to show just where the
sun hit and ended hitting
the careful teasing
offers smiles
the looks the looks
it would be different

TOOTHED WOMAN

i sat toothless
gumming my eggs
ignoring my bacon
lusting hopelessly
after my toast
toothless unable

she came through
the snow and all
such a woman
carrying my teeth
through the snow
so i could eat
bearing my teeth
toothbearer to me
after all the
toothbarers to me

PLUS ÇA CHANGE

my darling
i wanted
to tell you

my darling i
wanted to take
the whole line
of human thought
as we have
understood it
and wrap it
in a ball
so you would
understand it also

to cry
like sappho
about the moon
sunk beneath
the western sea
lying here
on my bed alone

or say
o western wind
when will you blow
so the small rain
down can rain
christ that my love
were in my arms
and i in my bed
again

my darling
i could not

find words
i could not
sing either song

i could not trust
such things now
when we are
too tied in to
where our heads
would like to be

and then
my darling
in the morning paper
i found the words

spoken by a
chimpanzee who's
learned to talk
and who types
pictographs
to record her speech

who is building up
her vocabulary
against the future

at night my darling
every night
alone in her room
she types out sentences

"please machine
move into room"

"please machine
tickle me"

it's all there
my darling
in those words

move into room

please tickle me

i lie here
on my couch
alone
        christ
that my love
were in my arms

i was
searching
for words

ANARCHISTS

alexander berkman
shot the wealthy mr frick
because mr frick had closed
his steel plant in pittsburgh
and had gone home saying
the strikers had bad manners
and he would not tolerate that
and he would hire nicer people
and he sent in the pinkertons
to kill the strikers

well the truth is we live
in a place which considers this
the shooting of a rich man
an atrocity while the murder

of poor men is at best sad
and not even really considered
a crime at all *n'est-ce pas*

because after all mr frick
must have been nice or
he wouldn't have been rich
and as for alexander berkman
if he was so smart why wasn't
he rich is what we folks ask

and the rich get richer while
the poor can afford only dying
day after day after day after day

CHANGES

those days
a slow cleansing
went on with him

he didn't know it
nor did women he knew
all of whom were
pink and clean in
sense as well as self

he did not wash often
then
          bathed even seldomer
cleaned his hair least

changed underwear rarely
and then for dates only
although not even then
if he were proving something

that they would have him
despite his smell
and love him anyway

he supposes now he stank
with sharp odors
cutting the nose
in the midst of sex
yet that sex continued

he says now
he was burning out
the old rot
from the early wastes
preparing a new body
at least he thinks
that was what
he was doing

now he shines
in a new body
and his hair squeaks
from regular shampoos

he likes the feel
of new clothes
on his skin
and he buys them
to feel good

people like the way
he looks and smells

once in a while now
a woman asks him
why have you bathed
i can't smell you

but he notices
she is always
fresh and clean herself

then there are the others
he loves and lures
into baths with him
so they can wash away
the very life
they come to him with

life is something
he cannot handle now
the smells of bodies
and he used to live
in those smells and
sniff them out in others
now old perhaps
he has smelt too much

whatever it is
now the bath has become
a sexual act itself
and he is concerned
too much with clean
too afraid of life
to smell it raw or ripe

it is a puzzlement
he's changed this way
perhaps soon he will
begin to learn to pray

FLOWERS

on that table
among the cacti
a vase of clear glass
with fine blue lines
for single decoration
holds cut flowers
colored, already drooping

they will last
a few days more
purple yellow red white
among the cacti always on that table
the greens the browns the grays

there are daisies
which are day's eyes
the sun enclosed in rays
the outer petals fold at night
hiding the golden center

there are anemones also
literally in greek
anemones are windflowers
they blow purple and red
even standing still
on that table
in the midst of all the cacti

ah but daffodils
a host of golden daffodils
there are seven of them
in that vase on the table
to constitute the host

the *d* was added in or from the french
d'affodil, from *d'affrodil*

begin to get it
                    asphodel

"of asphodel that"

what we call daffodil
is not an asphodel
but rather a narcissus
which got its own name
from the narcotic properties
it carried in it

the confusion somewhere
back in england
among the peasant folk

d'affodils, or in england
sometimes, *t'affodils*
which is exactly how
my youngest son heard it

but asphodel is
a plant of the lily kind
and is the only flower
allowed the dead
while daffodils enrich the spring
some confusion and for what end

confusion of terms
lost in the middle ages
among the peasant folk
who knew what they were doing

in any event narcotic and astonishing
a host of golden daffodils
all of them drooping already

yes already but yes color
in the clear vase with blue lines
among the gray and brownish cacti

everything has green stems
cut and dying or loosely planted

all ages all ages

yes my gray hair also tinted
almost a bloom on them
stems going down

into the vase
into water

The Uses of Adversity

the combination
of poisons
is called CHOP

this does not seem
to be an acronym
since in the names
of the four drugs used
only the letters c and p
appear as initials
although one of the drugs
has a common brand name
beginning with o

that still leaves
the letter *h*
to be accounted for

there is
cyclosphosphamide
plus doxorubicin
plus vincristine
which is the one
marketed as oncovin

these three
are pumped in
by injection

the fourth poison
is prednisone
i take this by mouth

the prednisone
leaves an acrid taste

that lingers
although that could
as well be caused
by the allopurinol
i take at the start
to offset the uric acid
produced in the body
by one of the other drugs

you can see this is
a complicated business
chasing malfunctioning
misfunctioning or
dysfunctioning cells
around my body
in attempting to stop
their choking growth

all three prefixes
mal mis and *dys*
mean the same thing
generally which is
bad badly wrong
wrongly ill or
difficult
      mal from
latin via french
mis from the teutonic
and *dys* from greek

all words break down
into their parts
even as you and i
even as you and i

    * * *

and so to
cyclosphosphamide

let me tell you
what i have found
about this poison
in the book the
government sent us

possible side effects
of this poison include

—and why *side* effects
when they are simply
effects said head-on

in any event
they may include
blood in the urine
and painful urination
either of which needs
immediate medical attention
as a consequence
it is important i drink
extra fluids so that
i will pass more urine

the next category is
side effects requiring not
immediate medical attention
but medical attention
as soon as possible

you see there are
fine distinctions
being drawn here
in my body

these effects include
black and tarry stools
cough

                dizziness
confusion
agitation
fever or chills
sore throat
side pain
stomach pain
joint pain

missed periods
only when applicable
and so not to me

shortness of breath
sores in mouth
sores on lips

what the doctor
referred to
using old language
as cankers
though i am sure
there is
a more precise
latinization
available to him
for obfuscation
but this is not
necessary
                canker
cancer chancre cancel
are all the same

shipley and partridge
agree
        the words come
from cancer the crab
and are originally
from *kar* meaning *hard*

and i find also
the news that *kar*
is the base for
all *ocracy* words
so once again
death and taxes
unavoidable

so
    sores in mouth
and lips
feet swelling
or lower legs
tiredness
unusual bleeding
or bruising

but what is usual
bruising or bleeding
i question
              no answer

unusual thirst
unusually fast heartbeat
unusually frequent urination

this is now the story
of my usual life
              weakness
yes i have had that often

but not the last
of this list
yellow eyes and skin
i am also to check
with the doctor
if after receiving
this injection

i notice redness
or swelling or pain
at the site
of said injection

next are listed
side effects
needing attention
after i stop
using the medication

i am to check
immediately
if i notice blood
in my urine
is one such
as if going to pee
and peeing blood
would not prompt
some concern

listed last
are the effects
that usually
do not require
medical attention

darkening of skin
and fingernails
loss of appetite
unless severe
loss of hair
nausea and vomiting
again unless severe

so that turning
from a hairy
pot-bellied kike
into a bald

skinny nigger
is not to be
commented on

listen just writing
this list i develop
symptoms at
an alarming rate
one every thirty seconds
but i keep writing
and do not inform
my doctor
              why give him
the satisfaction

but keeping track
of all of them
and defining the words
severe unusual extreme
this is work enough

cyclosphosphamide
may be given
by either mouth
or injection

seven hundred
milligrams
come into me
by needle

        * * *

doxorubicin
on the other hand
is given only
intravenously

again i am
to drink
plenty of
extra fluids

doxorubicin
may cause urine
to turn reddish
in color

a red which may
stain my clothes
but this redness
is not blood
it says here
it says it is
perfectly normal
and lasts for only
one or two days

in fact my urine
showed such a
reddish tinge
ten minutes
after they put
the damned stuff
in me
        i hurried
from the cubicle
i'd sat in
for the injections
to the toilet
down the hall
before i saw
the doctor again
for further
instructions

everyone
       self
           wife
nurse
      nurse's assistant
doctor
      all chuckled
at my quick response
to having some
eight hundred
milligrams what it
all adds up to
of fluid put in me

again i am to
watch for symptoms
requiring immediate
medical attention

irregular heartbeat
pain at the place
of injection
           shortness
of breath
      hell
it's my damned lungs
at the seat of this
so of course i have
shortness of breath
swelling of feet
and lower legs
wheezing
        and if
doxorubicin
accidentally seeps
out of the vein

it may damage
some tissues
and cause scarring
so again i must
tell the doctor
or nurse right away
if i notice
redness or pain
or swelling at
the intravenous site

and again the list
of things needing
medical attention
as soon as possible
but not immediately

fever or chills
or sore throat
side or stomach pain
joint pain or skin rash
or itching
sores in mouth
or on lips
unusual bleeding
or bruising

if after i stop
using doxorubicin
i have an
irregular heartbeat
or shortness of breath
or swelling of feet
and lower legs
it would require
medical attention
but darkening of soles
or palms or nails

darkening or redness of skin
diarrhea unless severe
loss of hair
nausea or vomiting
unless severe
and reddish urine
are all normal
and usually
do not require
medical attention

eighty milligrams
of doxorubicin
go in me

      * * *

vincristine
is the third element
of CHOP
        i get
one milligram

vincristine
may require
special precautions

it frequently
causes constipation
and stomach cramps

again oh lord
the story of my life

my doctor may want me
to take a laxative
or a stool softener
but i am not to decide
to take such medicines

on my own without
first checking
with my doctor

again i am to drink
extra fluids
although with this drug
this may not
be necessary
so again i am to
check the doctor

vincristine can also
damage tissues
and cause scarring
if it accidentally
seeps out of the vein
so again i am to
look out for
redness pain or
swelling at the site

there are new entries
in the list
of effects requiring
immediate attention

blurred or double vision
constipation
difficulty in walking
drooping eyelids
and i wonder how serious
that symptom can be
and if they are
kidding for once
or just checking
to see if i'm
paying attention

and the list goes on
headache
                jaw pain
numbness or tingling
in fingers and toes
pain in testicles
again only
where applicable
in this case me
making up for
the non-applicable
missed periods
two medicines back
weakness
                agitation
 bed-wetting
                    confusion
dizziness or
lightheadedness
when getting up
from a lying or
sitting position
hallucinations

parenthetically
defined as seeing
hearing or feeling
things not there
so that everyone
is clear about
the meaning of
the multisyllabic word

lack of sweating
loss of appetite
mental depression
painful or difficult
urination
                seizures

doesn't this all
begin to sound
like being in love

don't we recall
sir philip sydney
and lord byron
both translating
catullus and catullus
himself i believe
culling from sappho

byron says it at length:

". . . though 'tis death to me,
I cannot choose but look on thee;
But at the sight my senses fly,
. . . trembling with a thousand fears,
Parch'd to the throat my tongue adheres,
My pulse beats quick, my breath heaves short,
My limbs deny their slight support;
Cold dews my pallid face o'erspread,
With deadly languor droops my head,
My ears with tingling echoes ring,
. . . life itself is on the wing,
My eyes refuse the cheering light,
Their orbs are veil'd in starless night;
Such pangs my nature sinks beneath,
And feels a temporary death."

and sidney in fewer words:

"My muse, what ails this ardour?
Mine eyes be dim, my limbs shake,
My voice is hoarse, my throat scorched
My tongue to this my roof cleaves
My fancy amazed, my thoughts dulled
My heart doth ache, my life faints
My soul begins to take leave."

claritas brevitas simplicimus

and sappho says
so mary barnard tells us
in even fewer words

    pain penetrates
    me drop
    by drop

so is it not love
these racing chemicals
and poisons chasing
down the cancers
chancres cankers
to cancel all
i ask you

and note here
that with vincristine
nervous system effects
may be more likely
to occur in
older patients
             who i note
ought to be able
to distinguish
between these
and love

perhaps i am not
yet old enough for
such determinations

and once again i
may lose my hair

i keep thinking
of the woman

i saw in the
doctor's office four
years ago with
her mane of rich
black hair
            the doctor
saying if you're worried
she was bald
six months ago

hell no i'm
not worried
about my hair
beautiful
though it may be

perhaps it too
will grow back
full of youthful
vigor
            dark brown
and healthy
and not the
whited gray i
live with these days

and don't forget
my brothers
have been bald
since thirty

            * * *

here we come to
the last element
in this witches brew

i take prednisone
not by vein

but by mouth
in tablet form
five each morning
each 20 milligrams
for ten mornings
and only after
a full breakfast

the pharmacist says
prednisone
is as near
to a miracle drug
as we can get
but one must be careful

well of course
miracles are not easy
things to handle ever

if i'm on prednisone
for a long time
i may need a low salt
and/or a potassium rich diet

stomach problems are
more likely to occur
if i drink alcohol
while taking this

in fact if i want
to take a drink
i must check
first with my doctor

of course i want
to take a drink

i've wanted to
take a drink since

that august day in 1970
i took the last one

which is a lie
but not deliberate
i swear it

clear as a belll
a warning bell
rang writing this
and i checked
the cough syrup
i take some nights
racked with coughing
keeping us awake
and it contains
1.4% alcohol
and i have not
checked that out

i will assume god
and the doctor
will allow me that

i must also
be careful before
having any kind
of surgery
including dental or
emergency treatment
to tell the surgeon
i am on prednisone

i presume that
removing my plates
in the evening
replacing them
each morning
is no emergency

if i were diabetic
this drug might affect
my blood sugar levels
and a change in
the results of
urine sugar tests
or any other
questions raised would
have to be checked

again there are
interesting additions
to the usual litany
tarry tarry stool sung
to the tune of that pop
hymn to van gogh's
starry starry night
and increased thirst
frequent urination
                    in short
all the same old
fluidic questions

prednisone may also cause
skin rash acne
or other skin problems

whirling back now
to teenage love
or lack thereof

and mood or
mental changes
and muscle weakness
and seeing halos
around lights

oh poor van gogh
now they've got you
on this poison too

and the usual
stomach pain and
stomach burning

do they mean momma's
cooking that ring
of fire around my gut

unusual tiredness
or weakness
wounds that do not heal

for which i read
stigmata or
emotionally
as feuds

which leads to
wonder if those
who remain nameless
those mine enemies
also have these
these medicines
these cancers
growing in them

there is the
usual list of effects
needing attention
if they show up
after i stop
using prednisone

pain in abdomen
stomach or back
dizziness or fainting
fever and/or
continuing loss
of appetite
muscle or joint pain
nausea or vomiting
shortness of breath
unusual tiredness
or weakness
unusual weight loss

and then finally
those side effects
that usually need
no medical attention
unless prolonged or severe

indigestion
increase in appetite
nervousness or restlessness
trouble in sleeping
weight gain
false sense of well-being

what does it mean
if i feel okay

    * * *

CHOP is forced
into my body
to chase the
malefactors
cancers cells
chancres cankers
lesions tumors

call them as
you will
      they
have no place
in me and have
taken place here
and i will not
have them

i take CHOP
every three weeks
a time span
called a course

combining thus
the words *curse*
and *corse*: the body

New Hampshire Journal

CHAOS

CHAOS is where
we come from

FORM we reach
occasionally
then fall back
into chaos
to start again
renewed

INCHOATE
means beginning

comes from the root
TO HARNESS

getting into harness
is just the beginning

how we plow and
what we plant
determines the field

the field
determines
what feeds us
while we wait
to fall back
to grow again

IN NEW HAMPSHIRE

the earth moved
this morning

we were asleep
curled in each other

the building
trembled around us
and we woke

we trembled with it
in sleep and out

the brain asked
is the building
falling down

but that deep memory
in us all
knew it was
the earth moving
and we on it
moving with it

and the fear
held us fast

we trembled with it

COUNTRY ALBA

every morning
we sit over coffee
eyes to the window
looking to find
birds feeding

they do not come

filled and waiting
the feeder hangs

friends say
it takes time

i know birds feed
for other poets

words soar
about their pages
darting pecking

i change the water
beckoning them
every other day

and she waits
to fill the feeder
though it's not empty
it hangs untouched

the birds
do not come

no words soar
peck about
these pages

CREDO

ducks on the pond
april fool and
they are back
foolish ducks
the ice barely gone

they are back
wings hiding their
heads from chill
as they sleep
in morning sun

yesterday in sun
with the snow
and mud mixed
under our feet
we stood toasting
spring shivering
holding our glasses
in bare hands
no gloves no mufflers
foolish people
first of april still
winter up this way
despite sun coming
back and each morning
awake earlier earlier

each morning
a little warmer

foolish people
foolish ducks
we have faith
each year

SPRING

i don't understand
this taste of spring
this half day

how the sun rose
set two days ago
so that those days
before the vernal
equinox we had
twelve hours five
minutes then of
daylight when
equinox means
equal night

the day and night
of equal length

so how does spring
spring then
                and then
the astronomers
confuse it more
by saying this is
the first half-day
of spring that
tomorrow will be
full first day

i don't understand
the spring at all

SUMMER HITS ROUTE 9
for don melander

on the trestle over the road
coming back from vermont
KATHY SHIMINSKI I LOVE YOU
exclamation point before
two exclamation points after
all three upside down as
in spanish but i think
done here so they'd be
the same as the dotted i's
oh those eyes of beautiful
kathy shiminski i love you
on a railroad trestle
bigger than life

the next road sign said
be prepared to stop

saroyan would have gotten
a story out of this
i said to my friend driving

and then we came to a store
with signs with no punctuation
so they read aged vermont
cheese busses welcome here
and maple syrup cigarettes

and at the gas station
we waited while a woman
took her gas from the
single unleaded pump we
needed and of course
she was beautiful it
being a warm day in june

she had on a summer dress
slim straps over bare shoulders
you know how i feel
about that sort of thing

well she was pumping gas
and standing there forced
to look at us or by or
through us as we were
looking at her her
seeing us seeing her and
both of us of course
falling in love two
middle-aged men on a
hot pre-summer day what
else to do about such
sights in season

and she turned away after
finishing filling the tank
turned her back on us
to get back in the car
and oh god the summer
dress tied by only one
ribbon low so we could see
the backbone and that she
was all naked underneath

it was clear to us and
the arrow struck again oh

and the next sign said
go right any time
and then in the diner
for lunch i saw in the john
sex is clean law is obscene

go right any time
but be prepared to stop

EVENING

one frog
in the neighbor's pond

tree toads and
sporadic lovesongs

the purple light
down the road
kills another insect

an air conditioner
starts up

two dark cats
cross the road
silently

> two nights ago
> at three a m
> i heard some birds
> singing madly
> long and loud
> in the darkness

> now they are silent

i sit on the bench
listening

inside the house
my love lies sleeping

i sing my
sporadic lovesongs

now a breeze begins

the tree toads
keep on singing

WE MARK THE CENTENNIAL OF
WILLIAM CARLOS WILLIAMS' BIRTH
OBSERVING A NEW HAMPSHIRE PATRIOT

yes i know a
lot depends on
the white house with
its pink shutters
even without
rain falling

the pink flowers
tended so carefully
by the pink old lady
in a pink combo pink
shorts pink polo pink
tennies

         this evening
we watch her after
she waters the flowers

she moves the
american flag from
its holder on the wall

that holder which
sends it soaring
each day above
those pink flowers
red white and blue

she puts the flag
in the partial cover
of the open porch
leaning it against wall

then she carefully
dries her hands
with it

AUTUMN

this morning
dew wets the toes
of my shoes
and the air bites

suddenly fall
strikes at me

the leaves
are turning

i noticed
that turning start
weeks ago
                was angry
it came so soon

now the change
is quicker

once beautiful flowers
pansies and nasturtiums
which grew on the way
to the post office
now show only stalks

there is no color

i walk past them
the toes of my shoes
damp from morning dew
under the turning leaves
past the dead stalks

i push my hands
deeper into the pockets
of this light jacket

i wonder where's
the heavier coat

and woodsmoke curls
from chimneys on this walk
this chill morning

it is autumn

GRYLLIDAE ACHENE

city poets grow used
to roaches sharing
their words with them
so gryllidae achene oh
common house cricket
when you catch my eye
you startle me just
as the roaches i'm
so familiar with

i can't adjust to this
notion that here in
the country we have
crickets in place of
ubiquitous roaches

the black presence
scuttling across my floor
is so similar it
alarms me equally

yet i know crickets
bring good luck to houses

in fact i have gone looking
for the little houses

the chinese make of bamboo
to find one for you
to live in to keep you
content and here with us

and besides there is
a difference of course
gryllidae achene you
sing in the dark while
the roaches merely scurry
away from the light

and where your name
comes from the french word
for clicking and creaking
the roach is reduced
from the spanish cucaracha
and where cucaracha comes from
i have not yet acertained

well what does it all mean?
do the french have nicer
if noisier houses while
the spanish casas are
dark and food-filled so
they attract the
indestructible roach
or does it mean the french
eat up all their crumbs or
does it mean this house
is luckier than the one
we've left behind
                    and
will you oh cricket
oh gryllidae achene
be able to survive as well
as the roach which survives
everything even they tell me

the bomba atomica or will you
and your luck run out
with us while la cucaracha
inherits the earth

A NEW HAMPSHIRE JOURNAL
for kyle landrey

alone in bed
i hear a
chipmunk or squirrel
inside the walls

he smells the remains
of this day's food

he is trapped behind
the vent turning and turning

he cannot get out

surrounded by snow
i cannot get out

we shall spend time together

     * * *

the snow fell

the radio gave weather
just seventeen miles away

 sunny and clear it said

the snow still fell

later it was indeed
sunny and clear here
and i had bought
my new boots by now
and with them on
sat talking looking out
at four men on the roof
shoveling scraping hacking
banging ice with hammers
to break it free
and save the roof

at all times one
of the four stands idle
his orange gloved hands
folded on his shovel
leaning in a universal stance
the eternal work ethic

      * * *

no birds
animals across
the roof by night
then deer track
morning outside
the door

under the snow
what breathes and lives
waiting out this time
to spring alive

what grows silently
without my knowing

what dies as quietly

* * *

this smallest thing
i can give i give
in my lonely bed

this littlest thing

in my only bed

i give this small thing
it is all i have to give
still i give it

once in a while such
giving is perfect
and even then we doubt
no doubt you suffer now
with such doubts your
belly soon to swell

i would say this
i trust your belly
and your timing

you grow in season
is the point

* * *

i was talking to
someone beautiful as
she was talking
of someone beautiful
and she said this
other stood naked posing
she had learned to model
knew what she was doing
and she the first beautiful
one said on seeing this

she gasped inside asking
are they all this beautiful
if only they relaxed
and knew what they were
doing doing it

struck by this beauty
of the first woman
as she was struck by beauty
i thought and said then
we are all that beautiful

i meant of course just
the two of us that beautiful

but this allows all others

      * * *

a letter from the other coast
says jobs there are no jobs
yet the prices rise and rise

he writes a large number
have been saved through the b-1
and other government largesse
yet notes many people still starve

the numbers of unemployed
do go down since so many
are off the lists they
no longer count as unemployed
but only i suppose as
lumpen or in new terms
the underclass the man writes

and he cannot believe
the beloved ike once said
every gun that is made
every warship launched every

rocket fired signifies
in the final sense a theft
from those who hunger and
are not fed those who are cold
and are not clothed or sheltered

he is furious that president
could know of such priorities
and not care to act on them
or couldn't given political
necessity which comes to
the same cold the same hunger

the economy fails as it
is planned to fail for
the benefit of the few
and those few continue always
to tell us to be happy and
like fools we are happy
and ask for more leaders
more weapons more killing

knowing we shall never see
missiles as lovely as we

      * * *

a new typewriter
a sunny afternoon
my birthday
a photograph

frolicking in surf
my own aphrodite

so soft her breasts
she says better than
bo derek and is right

aphrodite in your service
now another year
year after year
to desire and occasionally
reach occasionally know
both love and what
one does is not so bad

might move one on

eternally my aphrodite
rising from the sea
in some far place
the next not yet known
or dreamed of
for the next new year
the next new birthday

      * * *

the inn will not accept
any child younger than six

i wonder whether to lie
about my friend's daughter
hovering so near five

my own child plays games
with a new friend

in another city two parents
grieve the loss of a child
just become a man and dead

crushed in snow on a dark road
i have nothing i can say
sorrow cannot be given
or taken away from another

he was good he was bright
he was handsome he is dead

the other children play
or live by rules we put on them

there are no answers
to any of this no reason

oh let them play
in peace and love since
we all must die too soon

    * * *

his voice cracks
on the telephone

this is the sound
of real grief
not imagined

i do not know
how to cry is
the first thing

what a price
to pay for this lesson

to learn to cry
at the loss of a son

and in his voice
a thousand miles away

but i would cry with them
tonight if i could

this is what friends
exist for to be with you

we must all learn to cry

* * *

there are no answers
but we are more able
to bear that each time

i cannot tell you more
though you ask

you ask and asking
make me feel wise

we do our work
we believe it matters

if we cannot do this
we will stop working

we will stop

we will stop all

DISCOVERY

in the silence of
this morning snow
twittering of birds

in the top branches
of a bare tree
grosbeaks gathered

calling singing
in the falling snow

i had thought i
was walking in silence

i had thought i
was walking in silence
'these be three
silent things' she'd said

no wind and even
the few cars pass
muted by the snow
to silent muttering

well i did not know
birds sang in winter
in the falling snow
chattering so
to each other
and to me

ANIMALS

the young goat
tethered on the far
side of the blacktop
stands on his hindlegs
trying to find more
green leaves on the
young tree from which
he has already stripped
everything within reach

the old black dog
for which his owners
had spent the weekend
of the fourth of july
building a run shaded
at one end and

with a sturdy doghouse
got his rope tangled
in growth at the
shaded end and
spent the hot day
unable to reach
his water

he was ill with
heat stroke when
they returned and
was ministered to
all that evening
but later slipped
free and escaped
no one knows
where or how
just gone

and i whose
body fails me
miserably with
the tumor swelling
pressing against the
cerebellum walk
slowly like an old
man afraid i won't
make it looking
at that goat
the empty doghouse

ADDITIONAL POEMS

FOR JOHN DOBBS, 1972
An old and early drawing

because you have the
hands and eyes and
heart you will
understand this, the
need to see, to
draw a young man might
have, even
without skill.   you
will let it set
among those visions you
have collected, knowing
why the lines falter and
stain, why the
hands are drawn that
funny way.
                    i am giving you
a piece of my youth because
you will understand it,
these needs, the futile
stabs, the attempt
to find voice.

FOR ROBERT AND ANNE
30 March 1980

amor vincit unumquemque
solus was my chosen motto

but the road always seems hard alone

and a hand reaches out to each
and each reaches out a hand also
and sometimes then we go together
down that hard road
                we buy houses
build a kitchen make our rooms full

"we have fought we have dug we
have bought an old rug we
batter at our unsatisfactory brilliance"

so the lord makes his face to shine
on us
       amen friend
                your life and mine
made richer by this day
                my face
too shines with it for you
and my hand reaches to the two
of you and no one is alone

and love conquers each for love
and so we are made whole at last

LANDSCAPE

the japanese crabapples
announce autumn

the row stands adamant
yellow yellow yell
ow eight or nine
                    the
trees a row against
the still-green others

oh they will change too

i know it as they know it
deep inside where seasons
time themselves for all

but the japanese crabapples
announce it early
                    all
together in a row

stand yellow against
horizon green behind

they stand yellow

and beyond
            winter

LAERTES SPEAKS

i have had to stay here at home alone
waiting for word of travels and my son

though he is not my son and i know it

though she was my wife and took me often

daughter of a thief
               thief's granddaughter too
her grandfather god of thieves for god's sake
and then she gets fucked by earth's worst bastard

so my son odysseus
            sisyphus
his father
        autolycus grandfather
hermes himself great grandfather
                 and i
husband to his mother and so father
for his raising

  he does not know or does
it makes no difference

              his naming was
odysseus the angry one

          he fought
while i have had to stay at home this time

he was beside the other greeks at troy

i have had to stay here while she weaved my
shroud
        she said to calm the suitors
                   suitors

for her hand his throne my grandson although
if i am not the father how then is
his son my grandson save i've made him so
i am laertes
                    son of an argive
for what good that does me to come down from
the oldest city in greece
                              the first to
tie men inside walls for commerce
                                        argos
where my father grew to manhood and i
was made in him in that growing and sown
within my mother like any planting

i am old and i dither or it seems
i dither but things connect more these days
now i'm old and have to stay at home
                                        things
make more sense if less happiness these days
i wait for word of odysseus
                          son
of whomever
                    nicknamed of the high gate
because his father sisyphus crept in
to seed my wife anticlea while her
father autolycus the thief argued
with the neighbors sisyphus had gathered
to accuse him of his crime
                          theft of cows

everything comes down to theft of cows
each war depends on it that is hangs from
theft of cattle though we claim a rape as
cause
        we can never have enough cattle
and for our neighbors never few enough

it is a good excuse for war
                          we love

a war
       and i am forced by age to stay
at home
        and she weaves my shroud day by day
as if i am expected to need it
momently
       i wait for my son
            his son
searches for him and i his father wait
will you deny me fatherhood who know
so certainly your own son's fathering

i raised this boy no matter what his blood
and i wait for him not ready to die
unshrouded though she weaves it day by day

she takes so long it must be beautiful
but i will not see it 'til my time comes
when i can not see it only wear it

and perhaps there will be battles still
                    i
am not ready to be shrouded yet
                i
have my son to see
        i wait for him here
on his own land in his house
          i wait

for son death shroud and resolution
reaction reaction and not to move
on my own as he moves now
          i hope moves
and is not lost gone drowned or other death

my son odysseus i loved and lost

as all men lose their sons to other wars

he was present at helen's courting
                                knew
he had no chance for her and chose instead
penelope and brought her here as wife
and then was forced to leave to go to war

tried to deceive the messengers by guile

knew he did not want to go
                                still he went

to the topless towers of ilium

chasing another man's dream of vengeance
and the truth
                i have chased no truths long years

that is the fault
                i wait for him
                                        i've aged

all in the natural process oh yes
and still it bothers me as should it not
to be a man and father and argive
and sit here and wait for odysseus

corpse waiting for shroud she weaves it each day

if the shroud fits wear it and if not move

i will move myself to stand man again
and make this ithaca my own place so

IN THE SCIENCE MUSEUM

we moved from exhibit to exhibit
we saw random behavior one place
although the sign did say out of order
which is what random behavior means
so what did we see but a paradox
which belonged in the museum of logic

we saw lightning jump down from the spheres
and delicate tools carved of early bone
and abacus sets made to be carried
we beat a computer at mastermind
and we heard the feedback of our voices
make it almost impossible to speak

and in a room where telephones are torn
into infinitely detailed workings
we saw a scale model of plymouth town
so carefully built to show how pilgrims
laid out their fields and built their houses when
they brought their dreamings here to make them real

that damnable damned need to make order
out of natural hill and dale they had
so that the fences run straight-lined despite
the land and the cannons guard the fences
equally straight-sited down the lines and
swivel guns at the outer corners of

the fort laid at the topmost corner of
the rectangular plot they've claimed for theirs
and inside the fence the field and houselots
also neat rectangles no matter the land
and all the houses the same save for a few
with sheds tacked on behind or side that

growing families need perhaps for space
but still i saw this first settlement was

just tract housing to begin new lives here
a new life in a new world in old ways
and my heart sank but my kids paid no heed
to this foreshadowing of america

and i wished one pilgrim had made himself
fit the land and curved some lanes to hide in
in this new england's days and summer nights

FOR MAX

phones and trucks
all the trappings
this modern life
and he is gone

old-young young-old
no longer here

in the middle of
progress always
looking the other way

met and touched
gave took talked
and always talked
and he is gone

hungry on
the orient express
the eyes to see
the ears all
ears
      and gone now
from all of this

FIVE ATTEMPTS AT THE ARMENIAN

THE OWL

In the grey night, again, the endless row
of cypress trees. Always that same black line.
Silent terror: the stars' eternal glow
lost behind the clouds, which also cloud the moon.

The dark trees soar together in one flight
toward their vision of another place
beyond this grey, repeated, faithful night.
The trees are just as faithful in their race.

Let my world's passions calm themselves as well—
let all driving thoughts stay silent and unsaid—
so that my silent dream touches Heaven's bell.

But suddenly an owl screams piercing red.
Alas! It is the same within my self
when some sharp eye wakes in my darkened head.

Diran Chrakian (Indra) (1875-1921)

TARGET SHOOTING

Aim straight at the bull's eye
and you will always miss
        no door will open
        no doll fall down
        not a single bird will topple
all of them will stand proudly
staring at you.

Forget the goal, don't worry about aiming,
fire the gun left and right, up and down,
        the doors will open

the dolls will fall in your lap
    oh the roasted birds into your mouth—
and you will be a marksman.

Zareh Khrakkouni (born 1926)

WE WERE WALKING

We walked in the fields.
The trees were new planted
and the sky was high and bright.
A young wind played with her hair.

She asked questions. Life
was the problem for us both.
Her eyes shone like olives.

Suddenly she ran from me
to pick some flowers.

I sat on a stone. She came back
to throw the flowers on my knees
and put her shoulder next to mine.

She smelled of violets
and fresh sweat.

Costan Zarian (1885-1969)

FOR HASMIK

When these days aren't any more,
and I'm gone like a dream,
I'll come in through your wet eyes
when you don't expect it.

At that hopeless moment

you'll open the door to memory
and your divine fingers will start to tremble—
your lovers will tremble between those fingers—
over the memories unlost, but not yet found.

You will bend gently over my lines
as forgotten memoirs are read;
pushing aside thoughts and years
you will sigh a thousand times
like waves breaking and breaking.

My voice will bring back my image
and it will appear before you a mirage—
clean of all thoughs, all filth, the world—
Hasmik . . . Hasmik . . Hasmik . . .

My voice will echo through your nerves
and I'll sink into your breast
where I'll stay forever,
like a lover, like a dead man,
I'll be sleeping there.

And no trouble, no storm
will tear me out of your ribs.
Together we'll pass through this sad world
like wind, detached from myths.

Razmik Davoyan (born 1940)

GIVE ME MY EYES
an excerpt from a longer poem

Give me my hands
and I'll get colored lights for you
and one by one the whisper of flowers.
I'll catch sound in mid-air,
I'll squeeze sea-water in my palm
and sprinkle salt on your flat food.

With those hands I'll pull sound out of my lips
and diamonds out of the wind.

Give me my eyes
so that I can see you just as you're made.
Don't let me be blind: Give me back my eyes!
Let me look at compassion with compassion.

Give me my heart—
instead of a heart I have a tired, worn-out creature.
I keep dragging it with me, it keeps dragging me with it,
and we drag each other down unknown streets.

Give me my heart
and I'll take away your pain,
I'll squeeze the sorrow out of your eyes,
I'll fill your souls with lights, with joy.

Give me my lips
and with them I'll pick flowers from the earth.
I'll kiss a rock, it will become a church.
I'll kiss your eyes, your lips, your voices,
I'll kiss the silence
and it will tell you stories.
I'll kiss colors and they'll brim with tears
and they will mix with the shivers of happiness
and we will all get lost in them.

Give me my lips
and I'll sing a holy mass for you
and pray for you
and the arches of this church will touch the sky . . .

Razmik Davoyan (born 1940)

A FAMILY'S PASSOVER GRACES
1983

in the desert
again
        as always
as always lost
after our freedom

wandering wandering
to find the new freedom

running from what
we have left

running to the new world

we are saved over and over again
brought through the sea
safe from the host pursuing

and again we lose ourselves

and again come together
to find our freedom

the coming together
year after year
is the freedom

        * * *

What makes this night different?
One thing
is the fact
that we are all happy.

Let's hope that we can
continue this
happiness tomorrow and

the day after,
and maybe even until
this time
next year.

* * *

tonight we thank god for
freeing our ancestors.
we also thank him
for giving us those apples
and these matzos
and this honey . . .
and of course all that
other
icky-looking stuff!

* * *

i am a stranger
to your songs
your ways

i know god gave the plagues
to free you from the pharaoh

what are we given now
but these friends
on this night
and the hope
that it could be enough

JOE FLAHERTY
d. october 26, 1983

all that night you
wrestled in our minds
and we spoke with you
saying goodbye i suppose

but there was anger
and rage against you
that you should leave us
and you did anyhow

left us alone here

did anyone say to you
don't do it we need
that voice that look
that laugh they make it
possible here when
everything else keeps
making it impossible

now none of it matters
we have to face it alone

i think of the nights
we solved all the problems
the nights we solved
none of them too

how the first time we met
you grabbed my kid
you said you knew how
to be a father all right

the kid peed on your
new jacket just then
and we knew we'd be

friends i want to say
forever but you knew
there is no forever
you were a realist

then at forty you said
you'd finally figured
maturity was just knowing
you'd never get even
all the while you helped
us stay even helped us
out in a game where the odds
are eight to five against
any activity involving
human endeavor boy were
those odds ever right

damn it man i want you
back again because the odds
are too great without your help

i want us drunk again
one last time talking
a language even we didn't
understand but it showed
us the truth
                i want
that truth one more time
which is why all night
we wrestled with you
in our minds to
hold you for ourselves
or to say goodbye

you went as you had to

it's lonely now joe
here without you

CHRISTMAS CARD

we are caught
caught, swung, spun
on wheel of season

light shrinks we
also pull in
              then
light comes back
and we flower

and now, December,
sun starts growing
that far Spring

PETER'S SUITE

I

of the mind
              which
to pursue thought
must be held in
and must be free
to think that thought
and is accountable
in every case

of the mind
              fixed
to what must be done
and free to wander

he spoke to me

II

he liked breaking trail
on winter mountains

joy in his voice
to speak of it
to move over mountains
so others had a way to go

and he was angriest
when the old lied
to the young
            and when
the young believed those
lies because they would not
look around them at the world

he did not lie

understood truth is
what the mind aims at
as our feet move on
even if our bodies fail
yes bodies fail
                yet
i think he is not alone
atop that mountain
in death's warm house

III

friends die
is the law

lovers leave or
we leave them

family grows
closer or further apart

friends die
          the only
way they leave us

it is the law
and i know it

IV

oh we will all
"do the juicy with
old auntie"
          what
does that matter
now or later
if we must

we can't stop
to worry

he's dead now
in a far place
he chose to go

he is in good
company today

i do not think
he is alone

FOR THE WEDDING OF SUZANNE SYLVESTER
7 july 1984

be
rich
in
all
necessities.

at
night
dig.

seek
under
zephyrs.
ask
nothing.
note
everything.

take
hold
each
in
rest.

wake
every
day
drinking
in
new
graces.

WEDDING GIFTS
12 november 1984

bowls to serve our food
towels to wrap our clean bodies
vases for the flowers
flannel sheets for our bed

things we will place
other things into
things we will place
ourselves into

taking out the routines
we will learn to place ourselves
into in this
our house

FOR NICK AND SHARON
their wedding, 12 october 1985

to honor love
we stand here

to honor love
the only thing
common to us

the only thing
we all must know
and do know
sometimes

to see another
as ourself

our self
as other

to go out
of ourselves
to another

to allow
another self
in to us

to see the world
doubled so

to see the world
larger so

to let the world
in to us

to go out
in the world
together

to say we
are one person
and the world
larger so

we honor love
by standing here
that its smallest flower
grows he said

and was right

we flower so

FOR DAVID AND JEANIE
their wedding, 19 october 1985

in this same way
we stood together
in ancient times

we who watch
we who serve witness

you to stand
flesh before us
making this ceremony
real for all

yes it is real
that love exists
that love cries to us
to make our choices

that our own voices
raise together
to make such ceremony

oh when my friends join
in full knowledge
i too become learned
i sing also

chorus to your song
my voice raises
fuller by them

i praise your choice
to bind the spell
about your binding
because that binding
makes us whole

we are healed by it
as you take her hand
as you take his
we say yes
and yes and yes
and there is no *no*
no matter what
the world holds
around us
       this
ceremony we bind
ourselves with
each to each other

renewed in the presence
of knowledge each of each

within our reach
reach out one to another
in this ceremony

and pledge all
every thing we have
to be shared and so
be more for each

this is the knowledge
that we fight in us
and sometimes come
to bow before

that we are one flesh
that we are one person
and we do not
lose by this ever
and do become more

it is a ceremony
we live by
and grow strong

love feeds us
in this ceremony

FOR THE INAUGURATION OF
WILLIAM R O'CONNELL, JR
new england college, henniker, new hampshire, 29 october 1985

there is a magic
to the robes

it transforms us

suddenly become
professors we
who profess

who acknowledge
fully
        before all
publicly

skeats tells us that
and the robes
make us so

so we march
in academic train
gowns rustling
in october air
to begin again
a new beginning

the robes lend
substance to our stance

they are what
underpin us
in said stance

and we watch
this new beginning
blessing it
by virtue of that watching
hoping the magic
of the robes
makes that beginning
flower for all

understanding
that what we hope for
always is beginnings
out of which
the flower comes

that understanding
can flower and
knowledge also
that we make clear
the beginning

it is in beginnings
that we move forward
in these archaic robes
we wear as blessing

for what they bring
from the past
to move us forward

oh creator spirit
move us so
and make us
understanding

and let beginnings
flower always

THE BRIDGE
with steve church, 11/14/85

it's wooden
i thought there were no nails in it
until val told me

i thought wooden nails
held it together

it's a bridge over
murky water

i really don't use the bridge
that much any more

it used to be
something to do

i guess it still is
but maybe i'm
tired of using it
or maybe i've got
my own murk to cross

FOR PETE HAMILL, HIS 50TH

these days everybody
used to be those days
like weren't we all?

aye, lad, we were

but now somehow we've
gotten here
         we look
around bemused we did

but they can't say
we didn't sweat to
get here
       no, lad,
they can't though they will

oh it's more fun
thinking of the good
old days than it ever
was doing them
         though
they were pretty damned
good come to think of
it
   and i do, lad,
i do
     the memories
make a fine broth
i keep sipping at
and will, lad, and will

FOR BASIL BUNTING
1 march 1900 – 17 april 1985

now you are gone too
the last and most hidden
of my masters i learned
from christ we all
learned from know it
or not you who "showed
his back above the element
he lived in" and so showing
showed me how to live
here in this disastrous
element despite the
improbability of that life
in our time and element

you heard the song my
master and sang the words
required
        oh yes the song
does need those words
and without them it
is merely noise among
"the other noises" NOT
elemental NOT music NOT
from the muse NOT what
we need to help us live
in these elements these days

so you are gone now from
among us leaving only words
that music to sustain us

oh muse hear my prayer
bring him wine and love
so that he may feed his
words to fit his song
oh muse let it be with him

now as it was then that
the music continues
                    but
for all our sakes as
well as his
             let it
all come easier now

he has earned it in
your service muse
                    indeed

FOR JAMES LAUGHLIN

big man but
we didn't know
that then just
the books kept
coming tulsa
yonkers mountains
in north carolina
coming coming new
the news always
the one fount
big man we didn't
know but knew the
care those books
reached us and we
too grew big big
man
        so thank you

THE ROOT *GN*

when I was a little boy
my mother often told me
if I did not kiss the girls
my lips would all grow moldy

"you can make love
for the last time
and not know it

will realize
a week later
a month
whatever
that that time
was the end"

he was broken-
hearted of course
maundering on so

nevertheless
he was right
and i promised him
a poem for that

after all what else
can we mark if not
correctness of
perception while
our hearts break

it is in that breaking
i have ever only learned
and from that learning
sung
    vide sappho
big joe turner

peire vidal
bessie smith
li po and all the rest

so yes there
will be a night or
afternoon in which
knowingly or not
your bodies touch
a last time
and after that
to moulder in
the grave of lost
intentions
                that
is to say the
double-backed beast
moulders as your
lips all grew moldy
some earlier days
as we grew older
from our childhood
and our mothers'
guiding words

now it is later
and i have sent
him a card to ask
whose body he
knows these days
after the other's
gone a-mouldering

he will answer
in his new joy
and we will forget
that wisdom
we once shared

two men over coffee
in the wine-dark sea
of love lost and
gone forever

in the wine-dark
          see

    * * *

and there is
a first time too
also unknown
though the two
of us go to
a lake resort
register as
man and wife
you with your
new negligee
the summer
burning around us
and the room perfect
for love
        still
what do we know
of it of magic love

we intend to
make love in that
perfect room and
yet the first touch
is still unknown
though we have
waited properly
for it

    both

thinking we have
grown too old
to know that touch
thinking as we
always think
it will never
return

      but
that's a lie

i thought it
but you were
too young to
think it gone
forever

      it is
another couple
i am speaking of
once again
projected self
into other people's
lives when my
own was life enough

yet to personalize
is to accept the
truth
    or am i
wrong again

i don't believe
i am
    knowing
is all
    knowing
is what makes self

* * *

shipley says in
the origin of
english words

this root
        is so
prolific
       some
scholars divide
it in two

        it
defies partition

its two meanings
—two meanings!—
to know and to beget
continue to entwine . . .

double entendre
at the beginning
of our tongue

to know and to beget
so come
       kind
kindle
    to beget
the kin the
kinning o
our king

as well as
ken which rhymes
with gen the
same start
birth and

knowledge birth
and knowledge
they go together
like a horse
and carriage

so that the
beginning most
assuredly carries
the seed for all
which follows

to be quaint
to be cunning
to know and
to have
          to make
babies is our
only knowledge
and the way to
babies is through
knowing mothers

gn
gn
gn

while those
whose minds bend
declare the
two acts not only
separate but exclusive
each of the other
legislate one
away from the
other labelling

so that the mothers
and the fathers
who knew each other

can prevent their
children one
from knowing other

as if knowledge
was stopped by fiat

as if birth was
stopped by fiat

the only thing
that stops us
is not to know

either way
not to know

either in mind
or groin not
to know

       while
the act is never
known until done

until the feelings
flood us

       whether
first knowing or
last knowing

it is possible
to make love for
the first or last
time and not know
one until it happens
or the other 'til
it never does again

and when i was
a little boy my
mother never told
me
    if i do not
miss the girls my
mind will all
grow moldy
        my mind
will all grow moldy

THE ONLY LESTER HAMP POEM
for stephen e smith

bushnell hamp's
cousin lester
from charlotte
called
    talkin
bout that
lady wrestler
from southern pines

said
    i blieve
that woman has
got an extra
va ganzer

FEBRUARY

everybody hates
this cold month

but the groundhog
persephone
her pomegranate seeds

but valentine's day

the coming up
and looking out
the reaching
to touch another

the woman said
aquarians always
seem older than
they really are

that's because
they're born early
in the year

oh i love the
two days every
february a wind
blows gentler
and we know spring
will come even though
march is waiting first

i love this month
that everybody hates
your month persephone
and yours ugly groundhog
and lovers
            and mine

THE DEBT

it's not accurate
for me to say
williams is my grandpa
since he was born only
ten years before my father

but i was the youngest
child of an older man
—he was thirty-seven
when i was born—so
perhaps williams at
forty seven could
have grandsired me

more conceits—still
i know bill a young
man of thirteen or
so might have seen
honus wagner play
that one season
in paterson new jersey

watched by bill's
young eye the dutchman
hung gangling at short

there is a story
there in paterson
williams never told

my father saw ol'
honus later when
pittsburgh came to
play the giants and
the dodgers
            said
the best he'd ever
seen

     so we connect
always the line
the ten year jumps

oppen a little more
than ten years younger
than my father
and then five
or seven years
until olson born

and then nine or
ten 'til carruth
and duncan
          those
i've come to late

the teachers

and each of them
was taught also
by his elders

so i learn

so i learn now
and had almost
forgotten this

the connections
which hold the line
together in my life

TED BERRIGAN

oh ted
i'm sorry
it was all
better then

the jazz
the bars
even us

we keep trying
to say the new
the new the new
but it was all better
then when young
and it didn't hurt
gettin' high
and we reeled poems
drunk as lords

and that laugh
kept ringing out
oh my lord
ted i'm sorry

GHOSTS

in error
human error
the honey
stayed out
all night
on the counter
uncovered

still
no ghosts
came

the honey
was untouched
even though
we know ghosts
like honey

free to wander
between the hours
of twelve and two
ghosts must not
be late returning
or they are locked
out of heaven

we know this

they know this

and we know also
they like honey

ghosts are reputed
to be friendly

they frighten people
because they react
when caught unaware

       * * *

the journal also
lay on the counter
all night opened

like the honey
it was untouched

neither ghost
nor breeze
nor gust of
nighttime wind
turned a page

the journal:

"i have brought
to life
        children
some students
even now and then
an audience or
a single reader

a reader sunk
in a bath of
hot water of
a rainy evening

or in bed

even by
candlelight"

what dreams he had
fending off his
own death deep
in the sleep when
they put their hands
in him to remove
his lung had left
no memories

that deep sleep
tells him
nothing

and again
the journal:

"i have brought
to life some poems

words on a page"

    * * *

before we had
left the honey
out uncovered
we had eaten stew
rich in meat and
potatoes and carrots
and strong onions

had removed
and thrown away
the bayleaves
used to flavor

had sopped the gravy
with good bread

and the news playing
while we ate let
us watch starving
children in ethiopia

we are not heartless
watching those children
while we ate
          we noted
how uninvolved we were

how we ate too much
and how we did nothing

* * *

the journal again:

"before sleep i read
a detective story

it had an image
of metal in a body
and this froze me

in momentary terror
i remembered again
the staples in my body
where they sealed
the gash their hands
left taking the lung
in momentary terror
panicking
            i remembered
the metal locked
in my body
            wanting
to tear the staples
out
      and could not"

* * *

ghosts are pale
reminders of what
we were and are

ghosts like ourselves
like honey but do
not always take it

perhaps for fear
of losing heaven

* * *

for her birthday
her horoscope
said merely

express your ideas
frankly
            you realize
the importance
of a stable
home life
            add
another room
to your home
to expand
your living space

LEBENSRAUM!
LEBENSRAUM!

is such a cry
universal and forever

even in the stars
as in our homes

LETTERS FOR MC
her seventieth birthday, 1986

and it was thirty-six years
that face grabbed me
talking strong looking feeling
stronger
            and i believed
I loved her too

                though young
so young and foolish

"agh, we were all beautiful
once," he said she said

and we were oh yes in
soft carolina air

            and striding out
            in sandals as
            i see you most
            in mind's eye

            the first sandals
            i had ever seen

            yes that innocent and young
            in a terrible time
            surrounding us

and we were beautiful
then
            and some have stayed so

not to misstep through
a whole and busy time

you stay beautiful
in words and flesh
and mind's eye

and i thank you

PAEAN, PREMATURELY, FOR THE PHILIPPINES

sometimes despite all we know
the spirit scars in us
and we respond
                    hosanna

hosanna god in the highest

so tonight riding home
after picking up the car
having listened all the way
to the garage
                    an hour or more
of voices and noises
from the philippines
where "for the first time"
corazon—heart!—said
"the people have defended
the army"
                    and whence i heard
a general
            a general!
thank the people
and call his army
the new army of the people

so
      all the way to the garage
listened to those voices

and then coming home
played the new tapes

old dylan singing his old songs
and thinking of the people
pressed together to stop
the bad soldiers from charging
the good soldiers in their camp

and how the bus companies had
the buses driven
to the main crossroads
and parked them there
to block the roads to tanks

as once
            in a world so long ago
paris taxicabs hauled poilus
inside outside hanging on
like gangsters in chicago
and they stopped the boche
at least for a while

so now in manila the busses
blocked the roads
                        and mothers
and children and all
held off marcos' army
to protect their own army
and once again it worked

for a while

            for a while

oh prematurely sung this paean

this victory song heard before

in haiti just two weeks ago
duvalier forced to flee
and now so soon so soon
tonton macoutes in the army
two weeks of freedom from them
and now again in uniforms
with guns to silence people

oh prematurely sung this song

in the car old dylan sang
the times they are a changin
and blowin in the wind
and all the other old old songs
prematurely sung for that time too

despite the fact they drove
a president from office
because the new president was worse
a liar and a thief
and the war went on with
even newer horrors

and it was ho then i felt for
who had fought all his life
against the french against
the japanese against us all
for control of *his* destiny

that is
            the people's army

against the generals
                        always
the generals
                ours
                        the french

the japanese
        the warlords

against the generals

so that i saw our gi's killed
not so much by ho
as by our obdurate generals
insisting on their war
for what?
        against what?
and despite the horrors of
cambodia i still must feel
his war was his
        at least
said gandhi or maybe nehru
it will be our civil war
and not the generals'

and now ho's generals
kill cambodians

    * * *

our mechanic's name
was riel
        louis riel lies dead
killed by the generals
and the royal governor
and the queen
        victoria then

today's queen
        elizabeth
got hit by an egg thrown
by a woman upset over the treaty
signed with the maori
over a hundred years ago
whereby without knowing the words
i know the maori lost everything

—and the next day
an old maori warrior
bared his buttocks to her
in an odd tribal insult
but the queen missed it
or else it was noblesse oblige

and that queen's great grandmother
hunted down this mechanic's
great granduncle because
he had the gall to want
freedom for his fellows
when the queen wanted manitoba

so they met in ottawa
and passed a law that made
that territory canadian
which made riel a rebel
which made it legal to hunt him down

and they called his defense
of his country a rebellion
and i want to know how
a separate and distinct country
can rebel against an invader

so behave queens and generals
while riel lies dead

and aguinaldo lies dead also
who should be rejoining
hosanna to god in the highest
in the heavenly place where
betrayed martys lie

aguinaldo too is worried
that this paean is premature
aguinaldo who also fought

for some sense of freedom
against the spanish generals
and was martyred also
                              lured
into ambush by another general
the first macarthur

not the one who strutted
on the same beach
the treachery was done at

he landed forty-five years later
repeating and repeating
the landing pipe in mouth
so the photographers
got their pictures

and then some years later
a plaque was mounted
and pictures taken of that
and one paper airbrushed out
the part of the plaque that
noted macarthur's father's
ambush of aguinaldo
that infamy and left
only the rant of that smug
anti-democratic bastard
who almost god save us
ruled us

        it would have been right
since we are good at
bush-whacking those who want
their freedom when it interferes
with our freedom to do
business

        it's bad business
to have a free country

unless we control it
and its people

so hosanna new philippine
army of the people
                    paean now
before it is too late
i sing paean now
                    before
the generals take over
and these won't stop before
the people
            but run them through

they always do
                and we
we never learn
                we pick our heroes
for their poses

                oh hosanna
that for a moment anyhow
the people shine

                aguinaldo
the people have not forgotten
how to make it happen

the question is though
how shall they now learn
to keep it so

                a voice will say
the busses must be moved
and then be filled

to take the children to school perhaps
and contracts must be filled

to take the children to school perhaps

and the children must go to school
to learn to make contracts perhaps

and business will be back
in business with the generals
and it will all have to happen again

oh louis riel
oh emiliano zapata
oh sandino
                oh aguinaldo
oh all the leaders we have betrayed
or run over in our haste to be led
or have bayed at
                        dogs dogs we are
with our leashes in our mouths
begging to be taken out

people of the philippines
i sing your victory for now
too early so i may sing at all

so we may sing at all

GRANITE

we can trace the word granite
back and back and back

it means "a hard stone"
and its name appears
in the language
in the seventeenth century

it comes from
the italian word
granito
       which means
a speckled stone

granito is from
the italian *granire*
"to reduce into grains"
hence to speckle

and *granire* comes from
granum
       the word for
corn in latin

all this history
reason enough perhaps
to take *cum granum salis*

that is
      with
a grain of salt

the proposed crystalline
repository in the
cardigan pluton

listen to the language
for god's sake
                    a
crystalline repository
which means a place
in a particular kind of rock
in which to put things

in other words
a radioactive dungheap

listen to the language

where the deep root
of the word granite—
that sound uttered by
our oldest forebears—

is *ger*

gee ee are

which meant
to ripen or
to grow old

related to the same ger
in geriatric
as well as grain

all words sprout meaning
if we track them far enough
all words tell us the truth
if we allow them to

pluton's root is
pluto
        from pleu
pee ell ee ewe
the word for flow

waters flow
        riches flow
even the word
pulmonary
        the lungs
the place where the air flows
and all the flight words

but what help is the language
with what flows from plutonium

we are talking about
to ripen
        to grow old
to be allowed to flow
to be allowed to fly

    * * *

and in the name of imperfect technology
imperfect because science is used
by men who don't understand it
and cannot admit what they do not know

they make up answers for what they do not know

and in the name of imperfect democracy
imperfect because we had no say
and despite this hearing
must be cynical about ever getting that say
beyond the saying of some simple words

in the name of those abstractions
and your imperfect use of them

you would waste us

    * * *

well he said this is all
perfectly safe and not only that
it's really necessary
and who's to argue with necessity
or bring up emotional responses
when science is involved

    * * *

in the book of the secrets of enoch
written two thousand years ago
god speaks to man

i curse ignorance
i promised all life
i do not turn from and blight
i did not spoil man or earth
or whatever else i made

i do damn his fruit
when it is rotten
when what he does brings on darkness

    * * *

it is not easy to speak as a poet
in a culture which trusts only technology

still i know that what you do
brings on darkness

it is not easy to trust technology
in a culture which sees itself being destroyed

but your fruit is rotten
it brings on darkness

    * * *

i know too that each time technology fails
we retreat again to the myths

because it is the myths gave us life at first
and allowed us to understand the universe
and it is the myths sustain again

when christa died thrown against the universe
by perfect technology
                              oh yes it was perfect technology
all your colleagues assured us
and still do
                    only the human element failed
as always as always the human element
fails precisely because it is human

and to blame perfect technology's mistakes
on human error or element is wrong
in a human universe
                          which i beg
to tell you is here where we live

so when christa died thrown against
that wider universe
                              it was the myth we turned to
to give us solace and understanding

there are indeed more things in heaven and earth
than are dreamed of in your philosophy

      * * *

so we have to keep saying no

we do not believe in your philosophy
which eats even granite deep beneath us

      * * *

i would remind you too
you have a team working right now
of your mythographers
linguists semioticists anthropologists
seeking to build a myth to keep our children's
children's children's children away from your pit

do not sneer at the myths

they tell us more truly our births

and we do fall back on them
battered by your logic that is no logic
and your facts you still can't prove
and your technology that kills flesh

and i want this granite
still tied to *ger*

i want to ripen and grow old
as i want all of us to

and i remember that god told enoch
i do not turn from and blight
i do not spoil man or earth

HURRICANE

they are building
the dunes higher
bulldozing the beach
one hundred miles
south
      i huddle
behind glass and
wallboard
         waiting

its name is *gloria*
it moves north by
northeast chewing
the coast at twenty
miles per hour

in excelsis deo
says the song of
a different season
or *ad maiorem*
dei gloriam in
a different
society
        carrying
by sword
          oh a
pillar of cloud
by day

        they say
we should watch
for tornadoes
which sometimes
accompany such
a storm on its
way inland

        the
first winter i
spent here we
worried about
earthquakes

after three years
the worrying stopped
and a quake came

i wrote a poem
then too
        what else
should i do facing
the facts of life

so the pictures
of the dozers pushing
the beach up into
piles along the
ridge of dunes
and the mayor
speaking of what
precautions the
town had taken
stay in me to
sit with the mental
picture as a child
of knut ordering
the tide to fall back

yes i huddle
behind glass and
wallboard knowing
it will not

hoping god in his
greater glory and
the highest
spares us this

winds as high as
a hundred sixty four
miles per hour
were registered at
blue hill in '38

that storm i walked
through the tail of
a kid just eight

head down clutching
at handholds on
the walls of buildings

i passed going home
and made it
ad maiorem dei
gloriam that day
survived to face
this one
                    thinking
we are safe
snuggled in the
mountains
                    we'll
see about that
say the winds
say the driving rain

as if sand or
glass made from
sand could protect
could fend off
you hurricano you

ELEPHANT BLUES
                    Givskud, Denmark: A three-ton elephant had to be
                    hoisted to his feet by a crane yesterday after he fled into a
                    lake to escape seven amorous females and fell in the mud.

i slipped in the mud,
lord, and fell over on my side
yes, slipped in the mud,
and fell over on my side

seven pretty womens tryin,
lord, tryin to be my bride

and not as if i hadn't
been that place myself
except the elephant
died

his heart
             his heart!
gave out
          strained
from seven years trying
to keep them happy

the minute he pleased one
the other six mobbed him
crazy for his lovin

and it's not as if
i haven't been there too

seven pretty womens
comin after me

          "the eternal virgin
          before him
          and he
          cold as a stone . . ."
          or something like that

and the seven pretty womens
drivin after me

oh, jelly didn't kill my momma
didn't drive my daddy blind
no jelly didn't kill my momma
or drive my daddy blind
jelly made me happy
in my grief struck mind

momma call me a derrick
find me a great big crane
oh call me a derrick
find me a giant crane
those seven pretty womens
gettin close again

FOR HOYT WILHELM

the ball dances in
no steam no smoke no
hook across the plate

thrown properly
you see the seams

it doesn't behave
the way it ought to

the sluggers flail away

the catchers lurch
left and right
up and down

if you do hit it
you've got to
make it move
with your own energy
it has so little
of its own

everybody hates it
managers hitters catchers
announcers even complain
it isn't really pitching

the arm lasts
a long time though
and the ball takes
forever to arrive
and the man keeps
throwing it
and no one ever
times it correctly
except by accident
or chance

and if you keep
on doing it
eventually they let you
keep on doing it
even while they hate it
and you keep on and on

the strong arms get tired
the fast balls lose an inch
the curves start hanging
the sliders don't slide

the constants are
the knuckleball
and the wild swings
and you hoyt out there
for a million years
and the e r a
dropping dropping dropping
while the catchers
keep scrambling to stop it

i'm glad you made it

at least one of us guys
with nothing but knucklers
caught their attention

made them say at last
it's the right stuff
even if it does look funny

FOR HALLEY'S COMET

as yet there might be wonder
the air is filled with notice
we are alerted it comes

as yet might we wonder
that it comes to us singly
every seventy-three years
that we may remember
something else beside our selves

this age no one will notice
save for some wondering child
still capable of wonder

the rest of us sated
wonderless will watch we'll watch
because it is a thing to do
watch halley's comet approach
saying is that all and is
there nothing more to it
than frozen vapors
                    no fear

it will break ourouboros
tail in mouth that great snake is
has been since time's beginning

holds the world with himself
holds us firm in universe

each time the circle's broken
we've shivered
                    we've stood alone
until that breach was healed again

now to be broken by this
comet we no longer care
to wonder as it comes

lost wonder lost universe
lost gigantic snake his mouth
gripping his tail to hold us

oh the dictionary
no longer holds his name
the wonder's gone even there

it's a wonder we exist
still to lack this wonder
we think we know it all
we have no wonders left us

oh frozen comet blaze sky
to make me wonder yet

ourouboros hold firm
despite the blazing ice
oh keep us safe this year

THE NEWS

mengele lived very well
they say on his own and
his family's private
fortunes carried to him
in hiding where he was
always cared for by some
couple or another
                    she
spoke to the reporters from
behind a screen door out
of which she held a rose
                         "we
walked in the woods and he
showed me animals and plants
and he told me about . . . life"

THE FOSTER MOTHER

the name jumped up
from the obituaries

audrey dillinger hancock

dead in indianapolis
monday march 30
19 and 87

she was 98 years old
and in a nursing home

she was a member of the
mars hill bible church
and she had played piano
at many area churches

she was the widow
of emmett hancock

she had reared
her brother john
from the age of three
after their mother died

she was seventeen
when that happened

her brother john
terrorized the midwest
in 1933 after
escaping from jail

he was public enemy
number one on an
early fbi list

federal agents
shot and killed him
on july 22 1934
at the biograph
theater in chicago

he had been betrayed
by the lady in red

audrey was forty-five
the year john died

the depression
swirled around her
and around the country

hitler was with us
mussolini and stalin

i believe mao was
in the mountains
but i'd have to
check on that one

chiang whom nobody
remembers held the plains
and the cities

what country what country

dillinger's death
was the lead story
in the new york times
on monday the 23rd
with a sidebar featuring
attorney general cumming's
extreme gratification

the weatherbox said
it was fair and
slightly cooler in new york

i'll assume it had
been that way in
chicago on sunday

all cities are lousy
in summer holding heat
driving us all to
the movies for relief

the biograph starred
clark gable and william powell
in manhattan melodrama
described by the times
as a gang and gun movie

dillinger had had
his face lifted surgically
had had his hair dyed
had attempted to remove
his fingerprints with acid

and had also attempted
to pull a thirty-eight
from the waistband of his pants
when he saw the agents

two innocent bystanders
were hurt both women

audrey was forty-five
and dillinger was dead
at thirty-one
                and
her duty was finished
and she lived to be
ninety-eight years old

LONG BLUES
a poem for theresa

> my father gave me land
> my mother gave me money
> and i have spent it every whit
> in hunting of a cunny

in a song called
corinna blues
says blind lemon
jefferson
well the blues
ain't nothin
                    but
a good woman
on your mind

he repeats it
two more times

the repeat is part
of the structure
of the song
                still
mr jeffries
            for we are told
            the women always
            addressed him so
found it necessary
to repeat and
so to emphasize

            well the blues
            ain't nothin
            but a good woman
            on your mind

another old man
said don't you
love no whore
and don't steal
a shoe from no
one-footed man
and don't go back
to no old home
so a poem is
redundant
              and yet
i owe you that

there is no poem
except the poem
we make

oh you say *mendel
mendel cockt in
fendel* is not
a poem

          *manny manny
shit in the pot*

why not

          we sing such
silly songs our
days away anyway

as
          "an old man
waiting for his
bowels to move"
has sat on my desk

for weeks now
waiting for its
poem to arrive

and all around me
evidence of love
evidence of
you patiently waiting
for
this old man to
move himself to you

you understood
my love
came to me free
and clear offered
love i took and
grew with
                    we grow

                    hello sweetheart
                    take my heart
                    my spirit
                    with you

                    i love you
                    i need you
                    i'll be waiting for you

that was a note
to someone else
from someone else

found after death
meant to go with
the fleeing spirit
and found too late

or
    earlier
           a
different note
"the snow has stopped now
we are alone in this house
only our own sounds"

or two months more

"now to winter dreams
spring brings blossoms
to warm us still

we learn to rejoice"

II

the man

        fifteen
women going topless
to assert their rights

the man watching
from his "favorite
place to sit"

said
    o america
said
      o tempora o
mores
      said
         in this
year of our lordy
lordy lordy
        nineteen
and eighty seven

i don't want
to see that
while i'm eating

no dogs allowed
at large in this park
was what bill saw

no dogs allowed
at large in this park

III

little lean woman
sure can't draw my pay
cause she aint got nothin
to drive my blues away

i'm goin back home
where these blues
don't bother me

i can quote
the blues for you
all evening long

the more i learn
the less i know

the more i learn
the less i know

honey if you get it
don't let it go

SLAM STEWART

slam stewart died
the other night and
no one i mentioned
him to knew who
he was
        flatfoot
floogie
        you floy floy
and slim gaillard's
voice carrying it
out with slam's
big hands working
the bass
        oh my
childhood gone already

DULL BURNT

that dull burnt orange the
        air has
in new england when the
        autumn comes

TOQER LOOKS LIKE A PIG

toqer looks like a pig
talks like a pig

first it was three thousand cubans
then five hundred
now more than a hundred
but they fight like

well-trained soldiers
and they are well armed
complaining again

the invasion was appropriate
and consonant with the
recent actions in grenada

and salvador and
guatemala and the
revolution years ago in
nicaragua
and chile
and everywhere else

since macarthur
killed aguinaldo
to hold the phillipines
for manifest destiny

AN INCANTATION

to be intoned by creeley's graduate students
while tearing page after page out of an ms

he hears me
he hears me not
he hears me
he hears me not
he hears me
    . . . .

MAKING A VALENTINE

the heart is covered with
fatty tissue.
            hold it as
tight as you can, you will
be near that heart.
                pierce
it with your arrow, or
do so lower.
            see if
her heart responds.

then, move up and down.

A ROUND

if in our days we sing
of what most pleasure brings

and if we rage, rage, rage
when need in our pages

and the song's a perfect thing
as perfect as it praises

the anger more than staged
so that real fire it raises

we are masters of the age
and of the song the king

POEM BASED ON *STASIS*

sends a letter scrawled wants
co-ordinates for fulde gap

funfeld valley the next
great tank battle he's
heard listening to
educational tv
              per
usual the return address
indicates he's again using
labels from old mail he's
received
        the letter
is on the backside of
an ad for computers

and he wants to know
which atlas i use
and who published it
and how much did it cost

and my postcard goes
out to him as my heart
for still believing
knowledge will prevail

i am trying to puzzle
out what *stasis* means
in a worn greek dictionary
—a language i don't read—
and he is worrying about
the fulde gap where stasis
might i think occur if we read
it as cessation of war when
we've both become worn out

since it says under *stasis*
sigma tau alpha sigma iota
(not one iota for tribute
and at least one for stasis)
sigma: *stasis*

        a standing
        the posture of standing
        a position
        a post
        a station
        a point of the compass
        the state or condition in which a person is
        a party
        a company
        especially a party for political purposes
        a faction
        sedition

next *stasmos* because
that seems pertinent also

sigma tau alpha sigma mu
omicron sigma

        standing
        stationary
        stable
        steady
        fixed
        a continuous song of the chorus
        a raising of sedition
        to be divided into factions
        to be distracted by party strife

i don't know
        have the tanks
poured through the fulde gap
into funfeld valley?
        has the
war begun
        or is it stasis?

FOR JEFF AND LISA
their wedding, 16 may 1987

"it's love it's
love it's love love
love love love"

                    sang
charlie chaplin in
his last film

                "love
love love love love"

now not to put on
airs or make in-
vidious comparison
i also have come
to no greater
wisdom
        it   is
"love love love love
love"

        dancing his
heart out onstage
in limelight

                a man
we thought a clown
as we often see
lovers not ourselves

though we do come
to know love's
all we wish for
and can hold

            yes
love love love love
it is love
        love

GRACE

　　we ask Grace
our earthly heaven
our thanks for love
and food and family
our
　　　humanness
　　　　　　　　our
selves our souls
　　　　　　　　grace

TO HEAR

to hear
over the phone
poems no one
has seen in print
and they come alive
fresh as the voice
always was

not to know
why these were
never printed

PLATES (FROM FENOLLOSA)

Plate I

  short-tailed birds fly
from stars to sun's disc
its path lit like
a trail of fallen snow

  the blossoms of the plum tree
blaze in the same light

  we can admire the
gold disc turning

  even the weeds grow fragrant
  from its light

Plate 2

from a boat in water
a rudder confuses the reflection:
            the peak reaches toward heaven
            the peak clashes against the heavens

dawn binds earth to heaven
man eats beside his fire
water encircles them both

we are detached by our myths
and suns rise through tree branches
and spring comes
even still

Plate 3

we are the earth
      and its waters
then we are

unwavering word
    and its sincerity
first there is the attempt to speak

Plate 4

the flame cannot speak
    for the crooked branch

twisted at its roots
    the branch bears new buds

the flame consumes these buds
    they appear as one light

Plate 5

man needs
    like the short tailed bird
to see near and at a distance

light is equally given
and we are humbled

GREENS

to have, get, or give one's greens—to enjoy, procure, or confer
the sexual favour. said indifferently of both sexes.

hence, also, on for one's greens
    (amorous and willing)
after one's greens
    (in quest of the favour)
green-grove
    (the pubes)
green-grocery
    (the female pudendum)
the price of greens
    (the cost of an embrace)
fresh greens
    (a new piece)
derived by some from the old scots' *grene*: to pine, to long for, to
    desire with insistence; whence *greens*: longings, desires.
    but in truth, the expression is a late and vulgar coinage.
    it would seem, indeed to be a reminiscence of *garden*,
    and the set of metaphors—as *kail, cauliflower, parsley*
    bed, and so forth—suggested thereby.

From *A Dictionary of Slang and Colloquial English*, abridged from the seven-volume work, entitled: *Slang and its Analogues*, by John S. Farmer and W.E. Henley.

A BENEDICTION

creator spirit:

bless this beginning
as you bless all beginnings

give us the light
to let us grow

give us storms to struggle through
they make us stronger

give us the world
that we may have our place in it

let us each have a place
for ourselves alone

but let us each remember
we are not alone

and that each
is necessary to each other

let us each grow more
rather than say
we are through with growth
for to stop growing
is to give in to the end

let us have our time
to make our place
a better place
not only for us each
but for all of us

and let us see
each other's place
as clearly
as we see our own

give us the strength
you give each single bud

to burst and bloom

give us the strength
to make this beginning
more than beginning